Cross Ownership at the Crossroads

The Case for Repealing the FCC's Newspaper/Broadcast Cross Ownership Ban

CROSS OWNERSHIP *at the* CROSSROADS

The Case for Repealing the FCC's Newspaper/Broadcast Cross Ownership Ban

Richard T. Kaplar
With an Introduction by Laurence H. Winer

Media Policy Series
The Media Institute
Washington, D.C.

Cross Ownership at the Crossroads:
The Case for Repealing the FCC's Newspaper/Broadcast Cross Ownership Ban

First printing May 1997.

Published by The Media Institute, Washington, D.C.

Printed in the United States of America.

ISBN: 0-937790-55-9

Library of Congress Catalog Card Number: 97-93547

Table of Contents

INTRODUCTION

At the Crossroads of Change

In its 1978 opinion in *FCC v. National Citizens Committee for Broadcasting*, the Supreme Court upheld the constitutionality of the FCC's newspaper/broadcast cross ownership restriction instituted in 1975. This prohibits common ownership of a radio or television broadcast station and a daily newspaper in the same community.

The FCC's regulation was premised on a dual notion of diversity—the need to prevent undue concentrations of economic power and the notion that diversification of mass media ownership promotes diversity of programming and viewpoints and thereby serves the public interest. This latter appeal to an interest in diversity in the marketplace of ideas focused on the only significantly available mass media at the time, newspapers and broadcasting. The Court's First Amendment ruling in *National Citizens Committee* was based on the FCC's authority to regulate broadcasting stemming from the then well-established scarcity rationale. Indeed, the Court relied heavily on its broadcast scarcity *bête noir*, the *Red Lion* case of 1969.

In the last 20 years, however, the media world has been transformed almost magically. The advent of premium cable services in the late 1970s spurred rapid growth of that industry to where it has become the primary source for the majority of American television households. Cable itself now is being pressured by blossoming direct broadcast satellite systems. Microwave systems, UHF and low-power broadcast stations, videocassette recorders, and emerging advanced television services all add to the burgeoning mix. And, in our increasingly broadband, digital world in which voice, data, text, and video are rapidly becoming integrated and interchangeable, on-line media services in cyberspace are the next frontier.

Largely because of these technological developments with their plethora of media sources and viewpoints, the old idea of electronic media scarcity, always a rather dubious one, is quickly fading. The Supreme Court in recent years has hinted broadly that it may be prepared to rethink this premise for its anomalous First Amendment treatment of broadcasting. Already there have been some notable victories in media deregulation. For example, the Fairness Doctrine, the preeminent manifestation of the scarcity rationale and once the *sine qua non* of a broadcaster's public interest obligations, is defunct and not likely to be revived. And, the 1996 Telecommunications Act finally removed the artificial statutory barrier to telephone companies competing with cable operators just as the Supreme Court was poised to affirm a slew of lower courts that had achieved the same result on First Amendment grounds. The outcome of *National Citizens Committee* itself might be very different today.

Even as these developments show, however, government deregulation and the Court's First Amendment media jurisprudence often can be very slow to catch up to technological revolutions. Such is the case with the newspaper/broadcast cross ownership prohibition which clearly has outlived any conceivable usefulness. To its credit, in the 1996 Telecommunications Act Congress directed the FCC to review biennially all of its media ownership rules, including the newspaper/broadcast prohibition, and modify or repeal any regulation that is no longer in the public interest. The time to eliminate this regulatory vestige of a bygone era is well overdue.

The cross ownership ban is hardly benign. As is often the case, what appears to be content-neutral economic or structural regulation of the media usually has troubling content-related implications. This is true even of government subsidies, generally the most neutral form of state intervention. The ban determines who is allowed to speak through which medium in a particular community and therefore forecloses speech much like a more traditional prior restraint. In its well-known 1945 opinion in the *Associated Press* case, the Court noted that the First Amendment "rests on the assumption that the widest possible dissemination of information from diverse and antagonistic sources is essential to the welfare of the public." But as the Court immediately added, "a *free* press is a condition of a free society."[1] Thus the court *opened up* the newspaper market to greater competition despite the argument that increased membership in the A.P. would give it monopoly power. Similarly allowing co-located newspaper/broadcast combinations well might stimulate beneficial competition in the modern media industry.

Moreover, the government's acknowledged interest in programming and viewpoint diversity as a basis for the cross ownership ban is a direct appeal to content that the First Amendment should preclude. As the FCC itself recognized when it promulgated the rule, "[media] ownership carries with it the power to select, to edit, and to choose the methods, manner and emphasis of presentation."[2] This power should be exercised in a free marketplace of ideas, as well as a free economic marketplace, and not one artificially structured and limited by federal officials. For, as one federal court recently observed, all too often government "intonation of the rubric 'diversity' is a thinly disguised reference to its preference for [certain] editorial content."[3]

As we know all too well from the often-sorry 70-year history of government regulation of broadcasting, the temptation to abuse power over another person's speech is difficult to resist. The newspaper/broadcast cross ownership ban provided just such an opportunity a few years ago. Rupert Murdoch owned newspapers and television stations in both Boston and New York City and was seeking to extend the FCC's temporary waiver of the rule in his favor. His *Boston Herald* was often critical of Sen. Edward M. Kennedy (D-Mass.). In early morning hours as Congress was about to adjourn, the senator had an unnoticed and undiscussed rider attached to a catch-all appropriations bill that prevented the FCC from extending any such waiver.

Murdoch was the only person affected by this provision until he was able to have a federal court declare it unconstitutional. Such is the danger of even seemingly benign, structural regulation of the media.

Finally, even on more practical levels the ban is counterproductive and should be eliminated. The last several decades have seen a substantial decline in the number of daily newspapers in this country. This threatens the viability of an historically important democratic institution that is coming under increasing competitive pressure from proliferating new sources of information. As early as 1970 Congress tried to alleviate this trend with the Newspaper Preservation Act that generated antitrust exemptions for joint operating agreements between competing newspapers to preserve the economic viability of a failing paper. Under certain financial criteria newspapers can share common production facilities to achieve economic efficiencies so long as they remain editorially independent. Similarly, Congress's main, ostensible reason for the cable must-carry rules is to preserve the viability of free broadcast television that it asserts might otherwise be threatened if local broadcast stations cannot rely on occupying a channel on their community's cable system.

If these are legitimate concerns, they more appropriately and beneficially can be addressed by eliminating the cross ownership ban and allowing available capital in the media industry to flow toward economies of scope and economies of scale with joint operation of co-located newspapers and broadcast stations. This should entail no necessary diminution in editorial independence or diversity in news, information, or program services. At the same time, the potential for monopolistic abuse seems quite limited given the highly competitive nature of the media industry overall, with growth and development of new technologies in fact providing, and always threatening, new entrants as direct or close competitors.

For all these reasons, this book's examination of the newspaper/broadcast cross ownership issue from constitutional, economic, and practical standpoints is most important and timely. The following chapters explore the history and original intent of the cross ownership ban, the decline of the scarcity rationale, the fallacy of the diversity principle, the rule's constitutional shortcomings, its effect on competition, and the need for repeal. If this analysis assists Congress and the FCC in a reconsideration of the ban and serves as a catalyst for repeal, The Media Institute's publication of *Cross Ownership at the Crossroads* truly will be in the public interest in the best sense of that term.

Laurence H. Winer
Tempe, Arizona
April 1997

---

[1] *Associated Press v. United States,* 326 U.S. 1, 20 (1945) (emphasis added).

[2] *Amendment of Sections 73.34, 73.240 and 73.636 of the Commission's Rules Relating to Multiple Ownership of Standard, FM and Television Broadcast Stations, Second Report and Order*, 50 F.C.C.2d 1046, 1050 (1975).

[3] *Time Warner Cable v. New York,* 943 F. Supp. 1357, 1397 (S.D.N.Y. 1996) (enjoining efforts by the mayor of New York City to force Time Warner's cable system to carry Rupert Murdoch's Fox News Channel), *appeal pending sub nom. Time Warner Cable v. Bloomberg L.P.,* No. 96-9515 (L) (2d Cir. ___).

CHAPTER 1

Origins of the Cross Ownership Rule

The Federal Communications Commission's rule prohibiting the cross ownership of a newspaper and broadcast outlet in the same market dates from 1975.[1] Having been on the books for more than two decades, it might be considered an "old" rule. But, in two important respects, it is far older than its 20-year tenure would suggest. Substantively the regulation is not merely old but archaic, adopted to respond to a communications industry that was about to be swept away in a tidal wave of technological change. And chronologically it did not spring forth in spontaneous fashion, but was the culmination of 50 years of federal concern over the potential of broadcasters to create monopolies of service and viewpoints.

Nor was this particular ownership rule alone. It joined FCC restrictions that barred, among other things, cross ownership of a VHF TV station and a radio station in the same market, ownership of more than one AM, FM, or TV station per market (the duopoly rule), ownership of more than one broadcast network (the chain broadcasting rule), ownership of cable systems by phone companies or television outlets, and ownership of more than seven AM, seven FM, and seven TV (five UHF) stations nationally.

By 1975 the FCC had figured out how to limit most types of cross and multiple ownership involving broadcast media. The newspaper/broadcast rule was merely the final piece of a puzzle the Commission had been assembling in earnest since the 1940s—and which the FCC would begin to dismantle in less than 15 years.

How this cross ownership rule came into being is an intriguing tale that involves some familiar themes: the government's urge to regulate a new technology (radio, and later television); a fear, held over from the "trust-busting" era, of economic monopolies; the ascendancy of "diversity" as a consummate First Amendment goal; regulation based on speculation and conjecture rather than facts or proven harm; and the inability of regulation to keep pace with technological change. Many of the other cross and multiple ownership restrictions have been lifted or eased in the last 10 years, most notably with passage of the Telecommunications Act of 1996.[2] But the newspaper/broadcast rule is still with us, perhaps no more than a regulatory example of "last in, last out"—or, more ominously, an example of the FCC's reluctance to relinquish its regulatory grip without a fight.

The rule takes shape

The origin of the newspaper/broadcast cross ownership rule can be traced to an FCC rulemaking proceeding, begun in 1968, which did not even address the issue of newspaper cross ownership. This proceeding dealt squarely with broadcast stations in the same market, and was an attempt to tighten the duopoly rules that already prohibited someone from owning more than one AM, one FM, and one TV station per market. The FCC proposed a much stricter course that would have barred a single entity from owning, operating, or controlling more than one station of any type in a market. No divestitures were contemplated under the proposal, so existing AM-FM-TV station combinations could remain intact.

The rules as adopted, however, were not quite as strict.[3] Some exceptions were allowed: The owner of a Class IV AM station serving a community of less than 10,000 people would be allowed to obtain an FM license, provided a television station was not already owned; a daytime-only AM station could obtain an FM license; and an existing AM-FM combination could be sold intact if there were technical or economic reasons why the two could not be operated separately. Furthermore, the blanket ban on television cross ownership would apply only to VHF stations. Combinations involving UHF stations would be reviewed (and presumably approved) on an ad hoc basis. These exceptions reflected conditions in the broadcast market circa 1970: VHF television and AM radio were the dominant players, while UHF television and FM radio were relatively weak and still struggling to establish market position.

On the same day the FCC adopted these broadcast cross ownership restrictions, it also issued a further notice of proposed rulemaking specifically to consider the question of newspaper/broadcast cross ownership. "The comments of the Department of Justice...suggested that consideration be given to extending the policy of the proposed amendments, in some form, to license renewal proceedings and to newspaper-broadcasting combinations.... [I]t might be in the public interest to fashion rules embracing divestiture and newspaper ownership, and we seek through the vehicle of this further notice to make a careful examination of the matter."[4]

Achieving diversity, the Commission said, would be the goal of any such rules:

> We have long been concerned with the particular problem of newspaper-broadcast joint control as an important factor in the overall attempt to secure diversity in the control of broadcast facilities. It has now become clear that the most significant aspect of the problem is the common control of television stations and newspapers of general circulation.... [T]he public looks primarily to these two sources for its news and information on public affairs.[5]

In the first of many references to the speculative nature of the undertaking, the FCC noted the importance it placed on who controlled sources of information, "even though there may be an absence of any definitive measurement of the degree to which mass communications actually influence thought and behavior."[6] Thus did the FCC proceed to solicit comments, undaunted by the question of whether the mass media truly had any effect on people's opinions, and therefore whether ownership restrictions in the name of diversity would serve any real purpose. Moreover, the Commission never offered a detailed definition of "diversity," leaving the term about as vague and subject to interpretation as the "public interest."

1975: The rule takes effect

By 1975, the FCC had reached a verdict: Restrictions on the common ownership of newspapers and broadcast outlets would be a good way to promote diversity of viewpoints and economic competition. Having received comments from scores of organizations, reviewed numerous legal and economic analyses, and heard two and a half days of oral argument, the Commission adopted rules that would not only bar certain prospective combinations, but would also require divestiture in 16 "egregious" cases. Apparently the FCC was not terribly moved by the weight of comments it received, since it acknowledged that "most parties" opposed the rule changes and only "a number" supported them.[7]

Nonetheless, the Commission adopted a regulation that can be summarized briefly as follows:

(1) The rule is limited to "daily newspapers of general circulation," *i.e.*, published at least four times per week. Collegiate papers, even if daily, are excluded.

(2) The rule applies to both radio and television outlets, including UHF television stations.

(3) Common ownership of a newspaper and broadcast outlet is prohibited in cases where the broadcast outlet's signal contours (as defined by the FCC) encompass the city in which the newspaper is published.

(4) The rule applies to combinations created both by initial application and construction, and by acquisition. The FCC would enforce this by denying a newspaper's application for a broadcast license, and by declining to renew the license of a broadcaster who acquired a newspaper.

(5) The rule was retrospective, requiring divestiture of at least one outlet in combinations deemed "egregious"—*i.e.*, common ownership of the only newspaper and only television station in a town (or the only radio station if there were no TV outlet). Other, less egregious combinations were grandfathered, but had to be split up upon sale. Divestiture was initially required by Jan. 1, 1980.[8]

The Commission acknowledged that it was taking an unusual step in applying the rule retrospectively. Not only was the action unusual, but it threatened to take an unprecedented economic toll on those who were unlucky enough to own the only newspaper and broadcast outlet in town. The FCC dealt with that circumstance in two ways: First, it took great pains to point out that the requirement was only a divestiture and not a forfeiture. Rather than cause a forfeiture or economic loss, in fact, the Commission said it would grant a temporary waiver if the owner could not sell the station at a fair price, or if it could be shown that separate operation of the newspaper and station would not be economically viable, or if it could be shown "for whatever reason" that divestiture would disserve the purposes of the rule.[9]

Second, the FCC advanced the rationale that the station owner never really "owned" the station in the first place. All he "owned" was a license from the FCC, good for only three years, that allowed him to operate on an assigned frequency. Thus, since the rule specified a five-year time frame for the initial round of divestitures, the Commission argued that this was no more onerous than not having one's three-year license renewed. It can be presumed that this line of reasoning was of little solace to the affected media owners.

One can only imagine the uprising the FCC might have had on its hands had it mandated the divestiture of *all* newspaper/broadcast combinations. Indeed, the FCC noted 94 such alliances at the time the rulemaking began, but said it recognized the need to balance its goal of diversity against competing goals such as market stability:

> We remain no less convinced than before of the importance of diversity, but this is not the only point to consider.... In our view, stability and continuity of ownership do serve impor-

tant public purposes.[10]

What the Commission did not state is that "grandfathering" is a popular technique of regulators to quell opposition to a regulatory scheme. Thus, by grandfathering all but a handful of existing combinations, the Commission effectively neutralized the most vocal group of critics. Still, the rule garnered much attention simply because of the precedent it set.

Local ownership rules change course

Following adoption of the newspaper/broadcast cross ownership rule in 1975, the FCC proceeded at full regulatory throttle for the next 12 years. Indeed, these dozen years marked the period of time when multiple and cross ownership restrictions of all types were most numerous and most stringent. In February 1987, however, the Commission issued a notice of proposed rulemaking in which it entertained the idea of relaxing two local ownership rules—the duopoly rule and the one-to-a-market rule.

Duopoly rule. Near the end of the following year (October 1988), the FCC adopted a report and order that dealt with the duopoly issue.[11] The duopoly rule, it will be recalled, prohibited common ownership of more than one radio station in the same broadcast service (AM or FM) in the same market. Technically speaking, the rule prohibited one entity from owning two or more stations whose 1mV/m contours overlapped. The 1988 action relaxed the rule to a "principal city" contour standard (5mV/m contour for AM and 3.16mV/m for FM).

As a practical matter, the rule change meant that one entity could now own two stations in closer geographic proximity, although the duopoly rule still prohibited common ownership in the same city. The FCC cited several reasons for its action: its experience in implementing the local ownership rules; its recognition of the geographic area in which most listening occurs; the discrimination against AM broadcasters caused by the original rule (because the 1mV/m signal of an AM station is not equivalent to the 1mV/m signal of an FM station); the growth in the number of media outlets that had occurred; and data from commenters on the benefits of multiple ownership.[12]

The Commission noted that the change remained true to the duopoly rule's original goals while offering some important new benefits:

> We believe that this approach best serves the public interest by fostering our continuing goals of promoting economic competition and diversification of programming and viewpoints while not unnecessarily restricting broadcasters' discretion and by enabling broadcasters and the public to take greater advantage of the benefits of common ownership of broadcast stations in the same geographic area.[13]

The FCC's report was careful to characterize the relaxation as merely a fine tuning of the existing rule, rather than as an abandonment of either the rule itself or the underlying principles of viewpoint diversity and economic competition. Still, this action was significant because it marked the FCC's first retreat from its position of maximum multiple and cross ownership rules. The regulatory waters had begun to recede, ever so slightly, from the high-water mark set in 1975 with the newspaper/broadcast restriction.

One-to-a-market rule. The waters receded even further a mere two months later (December 1988) when the Commission adopted a second report and order addressing the one-to-a-market rule.[14] This is the rule that prohibits common ownership of radio and television stations in the same television market. The second report did not abolish the rule, but adopted a liberal waiver policy aimed primarily at major markets and troubled stations:

> First, we will tend to look favorably upon waiver applications involving radio and television station combinations in the top 25 television markets where there will be at least 30 separately owned, operated and controlled broadcast licensees or "voices" after the proposed merger. Second, we will also look favorably upon requests involving "failed" stations that have not been operated for a substantial period of time or that are involved in bankruptcy proceedings. We will consider other waiver applications on a more rigorous case-by-case basis....[15]

These other waiver requests would be judged, the FCC said, on the basis of "the potential benefits of the combination, the types of facilities involved, the number of stations already owned by the applicant, the financial difficulties of the station(s), and the nature of the market in light of our diversity and competition concerns."[16]

As in the duopoly case, the FCC said the waiver policy was called for because of the growth in the number of media outlets and by data suggesting the benefits of cross ownership. But this "modest new policy," as the Commission termed it, served another purpose too: It would allow the FCC to assess the effects of new radio/TV combinations with an eye toward dumping the rule altogether someday. In fact, the Commission spoke of its "desire to act cautiously...to continue to obtain evidence concerning the ramifications of modifying this long-standing rule."[17]

Significance. The relaxation of both the duopoly rule and the radio/TV cross ownership rule was significant for two reasons. First, it signaled the "beginning of the end" for cross ownership restrictions, even though these initial steps were indeed modest. Second, and perhaps more importantly, it marked a change in the FCC's thinking toward diversity and competition. For one of the few times in years, the Commission acknowledged that trading off a little something in terms of diversity and competition might yield other and larger benefits in the public interest: "[A]t some point the benefits of allowing combined station operations may outweigh the costs of relaxing such ownership restrictions with respect to our traditional diversity and competition goals."[18]

Moreover, the radio/TV restriction grew out of the same rulemaking proceeding from 1968 to 1970 that led directly to the newspaper/broadcast proceeding from 1970 to 1975. In fact, the Commission came to refer to the one-to-a-market provisions as if they were the same measure adopted in two stages—radio/TV in 1970 and newspaper/broadcast in 1975. Thus, one might think the FCC could apply the same deregulatory logic to the newspaper/broadcast rule that it did to the radio/TV rule; however, the Commission remained silent on the newspaper question.

1996 Telecom Act: Newspapers left behind

Congress undertook a wholesale dismantling of the FCC's multiple and cross ownership rules when it passed the Telecommunications Act of 1996—but, oddly enough, failed to do anything about the newspaper/broadcast restriction. With this act, Congress dove headlong into deregulatory waters where the FCC had only tiptoed before.

The most sweeping changes were in the area of radio ownership. Congress directed the FCC to eliminate the cap on the number of radio stations a single entity could own nationwide, and to allow ownership of multiple stations in a local market according to the size of the market, as follows:

Stations in market	Number allowed under common ownership
45 or more	8 with maximum of 5 in same service (*i.e.,* AM or FM)
30 to 44	7 with maximum of 4 in same service
15 to 29	6 with maximum of 4 in same service
14 or fewer	5 with maximum of 3 in same service

Congress also eliminated the cap on the number of television stations an entity could own nationwide, provided its combined audience share did not exceed 35 percent. In addition, lawmakers told the FCC to conduct a rulemaking on the one-to-a-market rule as it applied to television stations, to determine whether the limit on owning a single station in a market should be kept, changed, or repealed.

The Telecom Act also extended the FCC's liberal waiver policy regarding the TV one-to-a-market rule to the top 50 markets (up from the top 25). Furthermore, it allowed dual networks (subject to certain restrictions), and repealed the statutory bans on cable/broadcast cross ownership and cable/telephone company competition.[19]

These were momentous changes. They far exceeded any moves the FCC had made on its own, even in its deregulatory heyday during the Reagan and Bush era. Congress mandated these changes to advance the public interest by promoting competition, and acted in response to the vastly changed market conditions of the 1990s. So what happened to newspapers? How did the newspaper/broadcast cross ownership rule survive, even as most other multiple and cross ownership rules were falling left and right? Certainly newspapers were a part of the same media landscape and would benefit just as surely from attempts to promote competition.

The answer, it appears, had more to do with political expediency than with philosophy. The House version of the Telecom Act had, in fact, contained a provision to repeal the newspaper/broadcast cross ownership rule.[20] But it was traded away in the heat of negotiation, never to see the light of day, or President Clinton's pen. Thus had Congress squandered an opportunity. The newspaper/broadcast restriction remained intact, an oddly out-of-place political "survivor" that now, more than ever, lacked a philosophical foundation on which to rest.

Newspaper/radio waivers. At this writing the FCC is contemplating a change to the newspaper/broadcast cross ownership rule that would involve a waiver policy for radio stations only. In a notice of inquiry adopted Sept. 17, 1996,[21] the Commission took note of Congress's interest in the matter as evidenced by language in a House report on the 1994 appropriations bill: "It may now be appropriate to permit the [Commission] to establish a more liberal policy with respect to waivers permitting cross ownership of newspapers and radio stations."[22] The House report favored a waiver policy that would apply to the top 25 markets and would leave at least 30 independent broadcast voices—the same policy the FCC had adopted in its 1988 second report and order for television/radio waivers.[23]

It remains a bit of a mystery as to why the Commission has chosen to entertain a waiver policy for newspaper combinations involving radio but not television stations, a point well noted by some of the commenters.[24] One could easily go further and ask why the Commission is not considering outright repeal of the entire rule. In the recent notice of inquiry, the FCC shuffles its feet and says: "[W]hile the Commission now clearly has the authority to reevaluate its waiver policy for newspaper-broadcast combinations it is without specific guidance on whether or how that authority should be exercised."[25]

The fact that Congress had, only seven months earlier, directed the FCC to relax or repeal almost every other multiple and cross ownership rule on its books ought to give the Commission a clue. So should the fact that Congress removed a long-standing restriction in FCC funding legislation that prohibited the Commission from repealing the newspaper rule. Yet the Commission proceeds in the most timid fashion, citing language in 1994 legislative history, as if it could not repeal a rule of its own making without a direct order from Congress. Clearly, stronger action is called for: The FCC should take this opportunity to repeal the newspaper/broadcast cross ownership restriction in its entirety.

Chapter 2

Diversity: The Great Goal

The justification for multiple and cross ownership rules of all types, including the newspaper/broadcast rule, can be summed up in one word: diversity. Time and again the FCC has asserted that the goal of these restrictions is to promote two types of diversity, viewpoint and economic. (Economic diversity, or competition, will be addressed in a later chapter).

Diversity of viewpoints as a tenet of political philosophy has more to do with the listener, and with society as a whole, than with the speaker. The listener who is browsing through the "marketplace of ideas" is presumably better served if he has a wide selection of viewpoints to weigh, and from which to choose. Ideas that are truthful, logical, and of benefit to the individual and to society are expected to rise to the top and drive out the false, the illogical, and the bad. The presumption is that a democratic society functions best when its citizens are well educated and able to make informed decisions about the conduct of government and other matters affecting their well-being. Diversity is an essential ingredient in this process because it leads to a pool of ideas both large in quantity and wide ranging in quality. Such a pool is necessary if a meaningful weighing and validation of ideas is to take place.

In this scenario, the speaker is of rather secondary importance. The speaker's role is to provide another voice, another viewpoint that can be weighed and either accepted or rejected by the listener. In traditional speaker-oriented First Amendment theory, on the other hand, speech is not merely a unit of listener input, but is celebrated and protected as a form of creative expression. The very act of protecting speech acknowledges that speech has value primarily because it reflects the worth, or "human dignity," if you will, of the speaker.

Thus, there is evident tension between the listener-based and speaker-based approaches to the First Amendment. As Craig Smith has pointed out:

> The original goal of freedom of expression and assembly protected by the First Amendment was to protect the right of everyone to participate in the marketplace of ideas—not to promote diversity in that marketplace. However, today some people would actually place the need for diversity mechanisms above the sanctity of the marketplace itself.[26]

This discussion inevitably leads to two questions in the context of communications policy: (1) Will the government favor a speaker-based or listener-based approach to the First Amendment? (2) Having made a choice, what methods will government employ to advance that approach?

With regard to the broadcast media, it is abundantly clear that the federal government has chosen a listener-based, diversity-oriented approach virtually since the dawn of radio broadcasting. In a 1945 ruling, the Supreme Court said in *Associated Press v. United States* that an underlying goal of the First Amendment is to achieve "the widest possible dissemination of information from diverse and antagonistic sources."[27] The Court reinforced that view in 1964 in *New York Times v. Sullivan* when it stated that debate "on public issues should be uninhibited, robust and wide open...."[28]

Perhaps the Court's clearest statement on the matter came in 1969's *Red Lion Broadcasting Co. v. FCC*:

> It is the purpose of the First Amendment to preserve an uninhibited marketplace of ideas in which truth will ultimately prevail, rather than to countenance monopolization of that

> market, whether it be by the Government itself or a private licensee.[29]

In fact, the present regulated structure of the broadcasting industry can be traced to the early fears of lawmakers and small broadcasters in the 1920s that AT&T's proposed common carrier model, called "toll broadcasting," would result in AT&T having both monopoly power and editorial control over the airwaves. Neither prospect would bode well for diversity. The government rejected AT&T's proposal, concluding that a marketplace approach could not be trusted to serve the public interest.[30]

Regarding our second question, then, the government's method of promoting diversity was set in stone at the outset and has varied little in 70 years: Government would impose a regulatory model on the broadcasting industry, and would enforce diversity by choosing who could speak and who could not speak as a broadcaster. This, of course, implied a government role in controlling program content, at least to the extent that government would award licenses to some and not others based on the viewpoints they could be expected to express on the air. The alternative or "marketplace" method of promoting diversity, *i.e.,* creating an economic climate and structural environment in which the widest array of media speakers could develop freely, was never seriously considered.

Diversity and the FCC

As the agency charged with implementing communications policy, the FCC was an early and enthusiastic advocate of listener-based, diversity-oriented broadcasting. It was a legacy inherited from its predecessor organization, the Federal Radio Commission (FRC). By 1929, the FRC was telling broadcasters to meet the needs of the listening public by presenting a "well-rounded" (*i.e.,* diverse) mix of programming composed of

> entertainment, consisting of music of both classical and lighter grades, religion, education and instruction, important public

> events, discussion of public questions, weather, market reports, and news and matters of interest to all members of the family.[31]

The FCC's definitive view of the First Amendment as applied to broadcasting did not surface until the early days of television, in a 1949 document titled *Report on Editorializing by Broadcast Licensees*:

> And we have recognized...the paramount right of the public in a free society to be informed and to have presented to it for acceptance or rejection the different attitudes and viewpoints concerning these vital and often controversial issues.... It is this right of the public to be informed...which is the foundation stone of the American system of broadcasting.[32]

This document begat the Fairness Doctrine, which from 1949 until its suspension in 1987 represented the FCC's most blatant attempt to impose viewpoint diversity on broadcasters. Thus, at least with respect to broadcast media, the FCC had set itself up as general manager of the marketplace of ideas.

Diversity and ownership rules. This quest for diversity found further expression in the realm of station ownership, animating all of the Commission's multiple and cross ownership rules. In the 1970 notice announcing the newspaper/broadcast rulemaking, the FCC expressed its fears about the role of newspapers in hindering broadcast diversity: "It has now become clear that the most significant aspect of the problem is the common control of television stations and newspapers of general circulation."[33] This was a problem, the Commission said, because "the public looks primarily to these two sources for its news and information on public affairs."[34]

When the FCC adopted the newspaper/broadcast ban in 1975, it summed up its diversity policy as simply "placing into many, rather than a few hands, the control of the broadcast medium."[35] This policy "is derived from both First Amendment and anti-trust policy sources," the Commission said, citing *Associated Press, Red Lion*, and other cases.[36] But diversity of ownership is not necessarily the same as diversity of viewpoint.

Ownership diversity as proxy. The Commission's concept of diversity is ultimately one of *viewpoint* diversity in keeping with its perceived role as manager of the broadcast marketplace of ideas. This is consistent with the FCC's belief, noted earlier, that the American broadcasting system is built on "the paramount right of the public in a free society to be informed...."[37] The Commission restated this position as recently as September 1996 when it said: "Like all of our multiple ownership rules, the newspaper/broadcast cross ownership rule rests on the twin goals of promoting diversity of viewpoint and economic competition."[38]

However, this presents a rather formidable problem. Short of becoming a programmer itself, or engaging in blatant and egregious censorship, the FCC does not have a legal way to mandate viewpoint diversity directly. That would require the type of pervasive and absolute authority over programming decisions long proscribed by statute.

Thus the FCC does the next best thing: It mandates *ownership* diversity as a proxy for viewpoint diversity. The Commission assumes that different owners will bring different editorial voices to the airwaves, resulting in diversity of viewpoints. As the FCC pointed out when it adopted the newspaper/broadcast restriction:

> The significance of ownership from the standpoint of "the widest possible dissemination of information" lies in the fact that ownership carries with it the power to select, to edit, and to choose the methods, manner and emphasis of presentation, all of which are a critical aspect of the Commission's concern with the public interest.[39]

Even the Commission's interest in economic competition is related to its desire for viewpoint diversity. "[R]equiring competition in the marketplace of ideas is, in theory, the best way to assure a multiplicity of voices," the FCC said.[40] Of course there is no absolute proof for this statement, and the Commission was prudent to qualify it as theoretical. Competition does imply more than one market entrant, and here again the FCC assumes that having more than one speaker will yield multiple opinions. But certainly there is no guarantee that the Commission's carefully chosen entrants will actually speak with different voices, or that commonly owned entrants will speak with the same voice.[41] And "requiring" competition is a very different matter than creating a structural environment in which competing and diverse entrants can flourish. Since the FCC's ultimate goal is viewpoint diversity, "requiring" competition implies that the FCC will decide who the competitors shall be, and will make those decisions based on the potential entrants' likely program content and editorial slant. Anyone familiar with the American tradition of a free press might say this sounds suspiciously like a system of government-controlled speech.

Scarcity as the basis for encouraging diversity

Nothing has done more to give urgency to the FCC's quest for viewpoint diversity than the concept of scarcity. The idea that the electromagnetic spectrum is a limited resource with only so many frequencies to go around is as old as broadcasting itself. In the early days of radio, this unchallenged belief in spectrum scarcity led to three corollary views: (1) that the spectrum was too scarce to be availing of allocation measures like auctions or lotteries, and of market mechanisms like property rights; (2) that the spectrum was so scarce that it could easily be monopolized by a single large player like AT&T; and (3) that the government was the most suitable entity to allocate frequencies and monitor their use.

These views were based, at least in part, on the idea that spectrum was somehow different from other resources because of its physical properties (you couldn't see it, for one thing), and because it was just "out there," like air, and thus seemed to belong to everyone, and no one. For these reasons, there emerged the "trustee model" of spectrum management: The airwaves were said to belong to the American people as a sort of national treasure. The government, as the representative of the people, would take on the function of managing the airwaves as a "trustee" for the public at large. As a part of this responsibility, the government would award licenses to carefully selected individuals and allow them to broadcast over assigned frequencies, provided they did so for the benefit of the public, or the so-called "public interest."

This vision of spectrum scarcity did not merely provide a rationale for government control of the airwaves. It also gave great impetus to the government's quest for multiple viewpoints in furtherance of its listener-based, diversity-oriented approach to First Amendment jurisprudence. The original "chain broadcasting" and "duopoly" rules were early attempts to enhance diversity by limiting the number of networks and outlets one entity could own. All of the multiple and cross ownership rules that followed, including the newspaper/broadcast restriction, were cut from the same cloth.

The Supreme Court embraced the scarcity principle as well. The Court's landmark *Red Lion* decision in 1969, handed down just one year before the newspaper/broadcast rulemaking began, enshrined scarcity as a rationale for the ages, or so it has seemed. In the process it affirmed a listener-based view of free speech and relegated broadcasters to second-class status regarding First Amendment rights:

> Because of the scarcity of radio frequencies, the Government is permitted to put restraints on licensees in favor of others whose views should be expressed on this unique medium.... It is the right of the viewers and listeners, not the right of the broadcasters which is paramount.[42]

The *Red Lion* Court emphasized that broadcasters, owing to the uniqueness of their medium, did not possess the same First Amendment rights as print publishers in having exclusive and total control over speech that was broadcast rather than printed:

> A license permits broadcasting, but the licensee has no constitutional right to be the one who holds the license to monopolize a frequency to the exclusion of his fellow citizens. There is nothing in the First Amendment which prevents the Government from requiring a licensee to share his frequency with others and to conduct himself as a proxy or fiduciary with obligations to present those views and voices which are representative of his community and which would otherwise, by necessity, be barred from the airwaves.[43]

In 1974, while the newspaper/broadcast rulemaking was in progress, the FCC reiterated the two key findings of the *Red Lion* Court: that scarcity still existed, and that the First Amendment rights of the listener were in fact "paramount":

> We believe...that the problem of scarcity is still very much with us, and that despite recent advances in technology, there are still "substantially more individuals who want to broadcast than there are frequencies to allocate."... For the present, we do not believe that it would be appropriate—or even permissible—for a government agency charged with the allocation of the channels now available to ignore the legitimate First Amendment interests of the general public.[44]

Viewed in the context of the times, the FCC's effort to extend cross ownership rules to newspaper/broadcast combinations should come as no surprise. The government's desire for viewpoint diversity in broadcasting was as strong as ever. Indeed, the Supreme Court in *Red Lion* had, only months before this rulemaking began, reaffirmed the right of the listener to receive information from diverse sources. Cross ownership restrictions had just been placed on television/radio combinations. Extending the ban to newspapers was seen as merely the "next step" in a period that was decidedly pro-regulatory.[45] And scarcity was still very much a part of the accepted wisdom; not only was it acknowledged as a controlling factor by the *Red Lion* Court, but it was cited by the FCC in 1974 as justification for retaining the Fairness Doctrine, another attempt at viewpoint diversity.

However, the times were about to change and media scarcity would go the way of vacuum tubes, but the newspaper/broadcast cross ownership rule would persist as an anachronistic heir to the *Red Lion* legacy.

CHAPTER 3

Why the Scarcity Rationale Can No Longer Animate the Diversity Principle

For the moment, let us suspend judgment on whether diversity is properly a governmental interest of such magnitude that it justifies a lesser degree of First Amendment protection for broadcasters. Let us focus instead on the question of scarcity, which, after all, has been the animating force behind the FCC's quest for diversity. If it can be shown that media scarcity no longer exists, then one must question whether the methods the government has employed to impose diversity in a "scarce" environment are still valid. These methods include the newspaper/broadcast ban.

Before we look at facts and figures, however, there is one underlying and unavoidable truth we must acknowledge: It is no longer possible to judge media "scarcity" only on the number of broadcast frequencies available. In the early days of radio and television these frequencies were indeed the sum total of electronic media available. But in today's environment of media abundance, we must look at the total range of voices available from cable TV, satellite services, and increasingly, on-line information services and the Internet. Over-the-air broadcast signals are only one means by which news and information enter the contemporary household, and their significance has shrunk dramatically. In 1970, for example, the major networks commanded an overwhelming 90 percent of the television audience. But today that dominance has vanished and the networks garner a mere 50 percent.[46] That is still a noteworthy number, but hardly the sort of which monopolies are made. Still, the FCC persists in regulating broadcasters as if they were the only show in town. For the purposes of this analysis, however, we will take the broader and more appropriate view of the entire media marketplace.

The explosion in media since 1970

The media landscape of 1970, the year in which the newspaper/broadcast rulemaking began, was barren and sparsely populated indeed—at least in comparison to the media abundance we enjoy today. In 1970, for example, there were 581 VHF television stations and 281 UHF stations (862 total). By the start of 1997 that number had climbed to 682 VHF and 862 UHF stations (1,544 total), a jump of 80 percent.[47] Low power television stations, which did not exist until 1982, accounted for another 1,180 stations by 1996.[48] The number of radio outlets also rose dramatically: from 6,995 AM and FM stations licensed in 1970 to 12,134 stations in 1997, an increase of 72 percent.[49]

Television stations affiliated with networks rose from 600 in 1970 to 1,181 in 1997. But far more significant growth took place among independent (non-affiliated) stations, which increased from 90 in 1970 to 534 in 1997.[50] Of particular interest is the number of television stations the average TV household is able to receive. In 1970 the average home received 6.8 channels—the networks plus 3.8 other stations. By 1996 the average home received 40 channels[51]—a choice of 37 broadcast and cable channels *in addition* to the three traditional networks. This growth is due directly to the impact of cable television.

During this time cable television enjoyed a rise that can only be called meteoric. In 1970 there were 2,490 cable systems passing 9 million homes and having 4.5 million basic subscribers. Contrast this to 1996, when there were 11,800 cable systems passing 92.7 million homes and having 62.1 million basic subscribers. In addition, 54.2 million people subscribed to premium services such as HBO and Showtime in 1996, compared to none in 1970. By 1996, more than 79 percent of cable systems offered at least 30 channels, while in 1970 only 1 percent offered more than 12 channels. Today 27.7 million viewers subscribe to cable systems that offer 54 or more channels.[52]

The growth in absolute numbers of broadcast and cable outlets has brought with it concomitant growth in program suppliers and types of programming. The increasing presence of independent (largely UHF) stations, for example, made it possible for the Fox Broadcasting Company to create a fourth network in 1986. In April 1987 Fox began offering programs to 129 affiliates (or "independent station partners," as it called them) two evenings per week. Today, operating seven days per week, Fox boasts some of the more popular shows on television including "The X-Files," "Beverly Hills, 90210," "Party of Five," and "The Simpsons." It has scored big in sports by wrestling National Football League coverage (including the 1997 Super Bowl) from CBS, and in October 1996 launched Fox News Channel, an all-news cable entrant. The success of the Fox Network has inspired the creation of yet two more broadcast networks—The WB from Warner Brothers and the United/Paramount Network.

Many observers, however, would contend that even more diverse programming is to be found on cable, where offerings include CNN, C-SPAN, ESPN, CNBC, MSNBC, A&E, Discovery Channel, The History Channel, and The Learning Channel. Local access programming on cable offers still more diversity in the form of city council meetings, local social and cultural events, and high school sports.

Other media. The growth in broadcast and cable television outlets is by no means the extent of heightened media diversity. To these traditional outlets we would have to add direct broadcast satellite (DBS) services, such as DirecTV, which alone offers 150 channels of programming; multi-channel multipoint distribution services (MMDS or "wireless cable"); satellite master antenna television systems (SMATV); and the ubiquitous videocassette recorder, now in 85 percent of television households. According to the FCC, DBS subscribers numbered 1.7 million in 1995 and rose to nearly 4 million in 1996; fast-growing MMDS systems were predicted to have 3 million subscribers by 1999 and 4 million by 2000, while SMATV systems topped 1.05 million subscribers in 1996.[53] None of these services existed in 1970.

Scarcity and the FCC

Beginning in about the mid-1980s, the thinking began to change at the FCC: Maybe there *were* more media outlets out there than there used to be, and maybe they *should* be taken into account when assessing media diversity. In 1985, the Reagan-era Commission issued a new "fairness report" updating its 1974 assessment of whether the Fairness Doctrine was still necessary. The conclusion: It wasn't. The reason: The media market had grown so much that there was now ample viewpoint diversity—that is, there was no more scarcity. As the Commission put it:

> We believe that the interest of the public in viewpoint diversity is fully served by the multiplicity of voices in the marketplace today and that the intrusion by government into the content of programming occasioned by the enforcement of the [fairness] doctrine unnecessarily restricts the journalistic freedom of broadcasters.[54]

The FCC acknowledged that the Supreme Court in *Red Lion* had upheld the Fairness Doctrine on the basis of media scarcity, noting that "the Court's decision was necessarily premised upon the broadcasting marketplace as it existed" in 1969:

> But in the intervening sixteen years the information services marketplace has expanded markedly, thereby making it unnecessary to rely upon intrusive government regulation in order to assure that the public has access to the marketplace of ideas.[55]

Based on this reasoning, the FCC said in 1987 that it would stop enforcing the Fairness Doctrine because it believed the rule to be unconstitutional. As it stated at the time:

> To the extent that the [Supreme] Court is concerned about numerical scarcity in this medium…with the explosive growth in the number of electronic media outlets in the 18 years since *Red Lion*, there is no longer a basis for this concern.[56]

Other diversity-based rules. The year 1970 was a regulatory watershed for the FCC. It was the year it adopted cross ownership rules barring television/radio and broadcast/cable combinations and began the rulemaking for the newspaper/broadcast rule. And it was also the year it adopted two other regulations aimed at enforcing diversity: the prime time access rule, and the financial interest and syndication rules.

The prime time access rule (PTAR) sought to increase diversity by setting aside the first hour of prime time (7-8 p.m.) for locally originated programming.[57] Network affiliates in the top 50 markets were not allowed to carry network programming (with the exception of news) for more than three of the four prime time hours, nor were they allowed to run "off-network programming," which as a practical matter consisted of syndicated reruns of situation comedies.

The PTAR was intended to strengthen the position of independent stations by giving them a competitive edge in the prime time access slot (7-8 p.m.); not only would the rule increase diversity in that hour, but it would help promote diversity generally by making independent stations stronger overall. In practice, things didn't work out quite that way. Independent stations did get stronger, but that had more to do with the growth of cable systems and must-carry rules. Network affiliates ended up broadcasting first-run game shows (like "Jeopardy" and "Wheel of Fortune") and the independents ran reruns of situation comedies. So much for locally originated programming and the hoped-for diversity.

The financial interest and syndication rules prohibited the three major television networks from holding a financial interest (*i.e.*, ownership right) in programming they obtained from outside sources.[58] The rules also prohibited the networks from participating in the domestic syndication of programming to television stations for non-network broadcast. At the time the fin/syn rules were adopted, the networks provided over 90 percent of the prime time programming aired by their affiliates. Only 90 independent (unaffiliated) stations existed, and these reached only 50 percent of the country. The three networks virtually controlled access to prime time, critics said, which decreased the diversity of program suppliers and gave the networks an unfair advantage toward producers.

After long and tumultuous histories, both the prime time access rule and the fin/syn rules were repealed in separate actions in the mid-1990s. The reason: The media marketplace had grown so much that government-imposed diversity was no longer necessary. Noting the growth in independent stations, cable TV, "wireless cable," satellites, and VCRs, the Commission concluded that repealing the prime time access rule would "not jeopardize the competition and diversity goals that prompted the Commission to adopt the rule in 1970."[59] The FCC's thinking about fin/syn was similar:

> The increased competition facing the networks and the new conditions in the television programming marketplace eliminated the danger that repeal of the fin/syn rules would impair the goal of diversity of programming.[60]

Also, the Commission in 1994 relaxed a number of rules relating to program log requirements and other administrative matters. The Commission noted:

> Many new video technologies...have begun, or are just beginning, to assert themselves in the marketplace.... The emergence of these new technologies, coupled with the continued growth in the number of television stations, will create an economic environment that is even more competitive than the existing marketplace.[61]

Thus, by the mid-'90s the Commission had taken further action on its 1980s realization that the media marketplace had grown much larger and more competitive. The FCC decreed, for all intents and purposes, that media scarcity no longer existed. Joining the Fairness Doctrine in the regulatory dustbin were a host of diversity-oriented rules adopted in the early 1970s that the FCC now found unnecessary in light of market changes. But noticeably absent from that batch was the newspaper/broadcast cross ownership rule. Presumably it was absent only because Congress had prohibited the Commission from using appropriated funds to reexamine the rule, and not because the Commission found some sustaining merit in such a restriction.

Scarcity and the courts

The *Red Lion* Court, hearkening back to its 1943 *NBC* decision, invoked scarcity as the rationale for imposing on broadcasters a listener-based First Amendment jurisprudence. But it also recognized that scarcity could well be a temporary market condition and that, if conditions changed, "there will be time enough to reconsider the constitutional implications."[62]

Four years later, in 1973, the Court again noted it was dealing with a changing industry:

> Balancing the various First Amendment interests involved in the broadcast media and determining what best serves the public's right to be informed is a task of a great delicacy and difficulty.... The problems of regulation are rendered more difficult because the broadcast industry is dynamic in terms of technological change; solutions adequate a decade ago are not necessarily so now, and those acceptable today may well be outmoded 10 years hence.[63]

Eleven years hence (1984), the Court again acknowledged that it was dealing with a changing industry and affirmed its willingness to review the constitutional implications of its stance toward broadcasters—provided it received some outside guidance on the status of technological change:

> The prevailing rationale for broadcast regulation based upon spectrum scarcity has come under increasing criticism in recent years.... We are not prepared, however, to reconsider our long-standing approach without some signal from Congress or the FCC that technological developments have advanced so far that some revision of the system of broadcast regulation may be required.[64]

By 1996, all three branches of government had recognized that media scarcity, in real numbers and as a practical matter, either no longer existed or might very well be nearing extinction. The FCC had said so in no uncertain terms and had repealed the Fairness Doctrine, the prime time access rule, the financial interest and syndication rules, and other regulations as a result. The Supreme Court had acknowledged since *Red Lion* that scarcity might well vanish in time, but still seemed to be waiting for a signal from the other branches. Congress, meanwhile, passed the Telecommunications Act of 1996, much of which was predicated on the knowledge that the media marketplace had become large, diverse, and competitive.

Still, it is not enough to satisfy critics by looking only at absolute growth in the numbers of media outlets, or at the abundant new media that have supplanted traditional broadcasting. We must also look at scarcity as it is viewed in the study of economics.

Scarcity and economics

A variation on the scarcity argument was articulated by the Supreme Court in *Red Lion* when it noted that, as long as there were not enough frequencies to go around, broadcasting would be a scarce medium. This view was reaffirmed by the FCC in its 1974 Fairness Report:

> This scarcity principle is not predicated upon a comparison between the number of broadcast stations and the number of daily newspapers in a given market. The true measure of scarcity is in terms of the number of persons who wish to broadcast and in Justice White's language, there are still "substantially more individuals who want to broadcast than there are frequencies to allocate." 395 U.S. at 388.[65]

This argument sounds rather compelling on its face, and could be used to justify scarcity no matter how large the absolute number of outlets. It begs the question, however, by confusing the concept of physical scarcity with the concept of economic scarcity.

Scarcity in the broadcast context historically has been based on physical limits—the idea that anyone can go out and start a newspaper because there is an expandable supply of printing presses available, but not everyone can be a broadcaster because there is only a finite number of broadcast frequencies. (Among other things, this argument ignores the substantial monetary costs of buying presses and supplies, hiring staff, etc.).

In economic terms, however, all resources that are not infinite are "scarce." That is, if something is priced low enough there will not be enough of that item for everyone who wants it. That is the function of pricing: When a resource is priced at a market-clearing price, only those buyers who wish to pay that price will remain, and at such price there will be enough of the resource to satisfy the buyers who are left. Economists would say that all resources are "scarce," but no resource is scarce (*i.e.,* in short supply) at a high enough price.

No one on the bench understood this better than Judge Robert Bork. Writing in 1986 in the *TRAC* case he set out the economic distinction clearly:

> It is certainly true that broadcast frequencies are scarce but it is unclear why that fact justifies content regulation of broadcasting in a way that would be intolerable if applied to the editorial process of the print media. All economic goods are scarce, not least the newsprint, ink, delivery trucks, computers, and other resources that go into the production and dissemination of print journalism. Not everyone who wishes to publish a newspaper, or even a pamphlet, may do so. Since scarcity is a universal fact, it can hardly explain regulation in one context and not another....[66]

In today's media market, there are plenty of broadcast stations available for purchase provided one is willing to pay the price. There is no shortage because broadcast stations, like all other economic resources, are subject to the principle of supply and demand. Licenses are bought and sold in a secondary market where the market value of a license can be determined fairly readily. In this sense broadcast licenses *were* scarce when the FCC first gave them away for free. (Lots of people would like to get something of value for nothing!) Likewise they would be scarce in a lottery situation if there were little or no cost to enter the lottery and the license would be awarded free or below market value. In an auction situation, however, licenses would not be scarce because there would be only one buyer for each license—the buyer willing to pay the highest price.

Those who invoke the economic scarcity argument (*i.e.,* that there are more potential broadcasters than frequencies) invariably neglect to mention that, in this economic sense, *all* goods (even printing presses) are "scarce." Furthermore, they neglect to take account of the secondary market in broadcast licenses which, by maintaining fair-market prices, ensures that there is no shortage of licenses available to buyers willing to pay the market price.[67]

This misreading of economic theory is a handy tool for regulators, however, because it allows them to invoke a "scarcity" argument in perpetuity, regardless of absolute numbers. Indeed, even at the time *Red Lion* was decided there was a preponderance of broadcast stations in absolute numbers: 6,253 licensed radio and television stations versus 1,754 daily newspapers.[68]

Scarcity and speaker access

The third way of looking at scarcity is in terms of speaker access. This goes back to Justice White's reasoning in *Red Lion* that spectrum is scarce because there are "substantially more individuals who want to broadcast than there are frequencies to allocate." This reasoning, however, confuses media ownership with speaker access. The ownership issue is addressed by market pricing, which assures there is an adequate supply of stations available to would-be owners (as discussed in the economic scarcity section above). "Individuals who want to broadcast" refers not only to potential station owners, however, but to a possibly far larger group of persons who merely desire to speak to an audience through electronic means.

Regarding television, the explosion of cable has made it possible for the average citizen to become a cablecaster through a variety of provisions: local access channels set aside by cable operators for community use; leased access channels that cable operators lease to outside programmers; and "PEG" channels, reserved for public, educational, and governmental use.[69] Far greater opportunities now exist in cyberspace. Everyone can become an electronic speaker and publisher on the Internet by creating a personal home page or participating in the user groups, bulletin boards, and chat rooms that abound. An individual potentially can reach more people on-line than by having a letter to the editor printed or even by publishing a newspaper. Thus, scarcity is no longer an issue regarding a speaker's access to electronic media.

Therefore, having looked at the question of "scarcity" in terms of absolute numbers, economics, and speaker access, we can arrive at a conclusion that should strike no one as startling: There is no media scarcity. Given the growth of traditional radio and television plus the advent of new delivery systems like satellite, MMDS, and the rest, electronic media outlets today number in the tens of thousands, versus 1,556 daily newspapers. (The number of newspapers has declined 11 percent since the *Red Lion* decision.[70]) In economic terms, broadcast licenses are no more "scarce" than any other resource, and a lively secondary market prevents shortages by keeping supply and demand in balance. Moreover, the growth in cable and on-line services has made it possible for every speaker to have easy access to electronic means of communication.

To state the situation in a shorthand way: In numerical terms, the absence of scarcity means there is a plentiful supply of diverse outlets and voices to accommodate the listener. In economic terms, the absence of scarcity means there is an ample supply of media outlets (including broadcast stations) available to willing buyers who wish to be speakers. In speaker access terms, the absence of scarcity means there are ample means for a speaker to communicate electronically without having to buy a media outlet.

Since there is no media scarcity, the government's interest in imposing a regulatory regime on broadcasters (and newspaper owners) to achieve diversity loses all urgency. There is simply no reason to regulate diversity when a large and competitive media marketplace is already offering abundant diversity on its own. Given these conditions, it seems almost too obvious to say that there is no need for a newspaper/broadcast cross ownership ban.

CHAPTER 4

The First Amendment Threat to Publishers and Broadcasters

Mounting a First Amendment challenge to the newspaper/broadcast cross ownership rule is still considered a questionable if not futile undertaking in some quarters. The reason: The Supreme Court has already considered such a challenge and found the cross ownership ban to be constitutional.

That might be the end of the discussion except for one thing: The Court's primary rationale for upholding the ban was the scarcity of broadcast frequencies. This was not a surprising outcome at the time, considering the decision was handed down in 1978—less than a decade after *Red Lion.* As we have seen in the previous chapter, however, media scarcity does not exist today. How would the courts react to a First Amendment argument now, and how might the lack of scarcity turn the entire matter on its head?

FCC v. National Citizens Committee for Broadcasting

The newspaper/broadcast cross ownership rule reached the Supreme Court just three years after it was adopted.[71] The U.S. Court of Appeals for the D.C. Circuit had upheld the prospective ban on new combinations, but ruled that all existing combinations should be broken up as well—not merely the 16 "egregious cases" cited by the FCC.

The Supreme Court upheld the prospective ban but agreed with the FCC that it was permissible to "grandfather" most existing combinations; essentially the Court kept the rule intact as adopted by the Commission. Along the way, however, the Court made some noteworthy points about the First Amendment rights of publishers who wished to be broadcasters. *Red Lion* figured prominently in the discussion.

Underlying the Court's position was the "fundamental proposition" articulated in *Red Lion* "that there is no 'unabridgeable First Amendment right to broadcast comparable to the right of every individual to speak, write, or publish.'"[72] The Court took note of the broadcast spectrum's "physical limitations" and "finite number of frequencies":

> In light of this physical scarcity, Government allocation and regulation of broadcast frequencies are essential.... No one here questions the need for such allocation and regulation, and, given that need, we see nothing in the First Amendment to prevent the Commission from allocating licenses so as to promote the "public interest" in diversification of the mass communications media.[73]

Citing a rather Orwellian turn of phrase from its 1943 *NBC* decision that it reiterated in *Red Lion*, the Court noted that "to deny a station license because 'the public interest' requires it 'is not a denial of free speech.'"[74] The Court also rejected arguments raised by the National Association of Broadcasters and the American Newspaper Publishers Association that the rule unconstitutionally conditioned "receipt of a broadcast license upon forfeiture of the right to publish a newspaper," and that the Commission had "unfairly 'singled out' newspaper owners for more stringent treatment than other license applicants."[75]

Returning to the scarcity theme, the Court characterized the rule as a "reasonable means" of promoting diversity, given the fact that the Commission was "forced to 'choose among applicants for the same [scarce] facilities.'"[76]

In short, *National Citizens Committee* was the newspaper/broadcast cross ownership version of *Red Lion*. How might the Court approach the matter today, given the decline of the scarcity rationale? The Court acknowledged in *Turner Broadcasting* that the "less rigorous standard of scrutiny" of *Red Lion* was justified by "the unique physical limitations of the broadcast medium."[77] If the Court concurred that those unique limitations no longer applied, then the cross ownership ban would have to be judged by a stricter standard—either strict scrutiny (if the ban is content specific) or intermediate scrutiny (if the ban is content neutral).

A case can be made that the cross ownership rule is content or speaker specific. But let us say, for the sake of argument, that the Court found the rule content neutral and thus subject to intermediate scrutiny. (The Court did, in fact, say in *National Citizens Committee* that the rule was "not content related."[78]) To withstand constitutional scrutiny, the rule would have to meet the four-part *O'Brien* test:

- The regulation must be within the constitutional power of the government.
- It must further an important or substantial governmental interest.
- The governmental interest must be unrelated to the suppression of free expression.
- The incidental restriction on alleged First Amendment freedoms must be no greater than is essential to the furtherance of that interest.[79]

Regarding part one, the Court has held repeatedly (and specifically in *National Citizens Committee*) that the FCC possesses rulemaking authority in the realm of broadcasting.[80] For part two, it would have to be shown that the cross ownership rule's stated goals, promoting viewpoint diversity and economic competition, further a substantial governmental interest. The *Turner* Court has already articulated such an interest:

> [A]ssuring that the public has access to a multiplicity of information sources is a governmental purpose of the highest order, for it promotes values central to the First Amendment....

> Government's interest in eliminating restraints on fair competition is always substantial, even when the individuals or entities subject to particular regulations are engaged in expressive activity protected by the First Amendment.[81]

Whether or not the newspaper/broadcast ban furthers those interests is another matter altogether. Because the ban implicates First Amendment rights, it must be based on a factual record in response to a documented problem, as the Court stated in *Turner* (and recently reaffirmed in *44 Liquormart, Inc. v. Rhode Island*):

> When the Government defends a regulation on speech as a means to redress past harms or prevent anticipated harms, it must...demonstrate that the recited harms are real, not merely conjectural, and that the regulation will in fact alleviate these harms in a direct and material way.[82]

When it initiated the cross ownership rulemaking, however, the FCC noted "an absence of any definitive measurement of the degree to which mass communications actually influence thought and behavior."[83] And when it adopted the rule in 1975 the Commission stated "it is not necessary to have proof of abuses before we can act," and later noted that "[t]he rules are not in the least premised on the existence of improprieties in the operation of the media holdings."[84]

The factual record, then, was sketchy at best regarding any real harms or abuses stemming from cross ownership—not to mention the extent to which the newspaper/broadcast ban might actually enhance viewpoint diversity. Indeed, the *NCCB* Court referred to the "inconclusiveness of the rulemaking record" and said the FCC "was entitled to rely on its judgment" under a relaxed standard of scrutiny.[85] It is difficult to imagine that an evidentiary record could be compiled today that would satisfy part two of *O'Brien*, or that the courts would be as deferential to the Commission's judgment as they were two decades ago under relaxed scrutiny.

Part three of the *O'Brien* test, that "the governmental interest must be unrelated to the suppression of free expression," would pose an interesting challenge to the newspaper/broadcast ban under heightened scrutiny. Clearly, the governmental interest in diversity is *directly* related here to the suppression of free expression.

Suppressing speech is precisely the purpose of an ownership ban that promotes viewpoint diversity by giving voice to certain types of speakers by stifling others. To impose diversity on the media marketplace of ideas, the government must necessarily suppress the free expression of certain speakers by denying them an opportunity to own an additional media outlet of their choosing.

We would also want to consider the Supreme Court's holding in *Buckley v. Valeo*, that "the concept that government may restrict the speech of some elements of our society in order to enhance the relative voice of others is wholly foreign to the First Amendment...."[86] But that is precisely what the newspaper/broadcast ban does: It creates a "privileged class" of speakers comprising those who do not already own a newspaper in the market where they wish to acquire a broadcast outlet, and vice versa. Those who already own an outlet become, in effect, a disfavored class of speakers whose further speaking opportunities are proscribed by the FCC.

Part four, that the restriction must be "no greater than is essential," would likewise pose a challenge. One would be hard pressed to argue that a regulation affecting virtually all of the country's daily newspapers, television stations, and radio outlets is a "narrowly tailored" way to enhance diversity. Other, less restrictive means can be found; for example, the government could promote diversity by easing market entry and taking other steps to encourage a larger and more robust communications industry. An analogy can be found in cable television: The number of cable voices became much larger and more diverse when Congress deregulated that industry beginning in the late 1970s, undoing years of structural barriers to growth and competition.[87]

Moreover, as the FCC observed in *Syracuse Peace Council*, when developments render a regulation "unnecessary to insure the public's access to viewpoint diversity, it is no longer narrowly tailored to meet a substantial governmental interest."[88] Given the dramatic growth in the size and diversity of the media marketplace since 1975, it is hard to see how the newspaper/broadcast ban could be considered "narrowly tailored" under the *Syracuse* criterion.

Other cases. Two recent appeals court cases show how difficult it is for a cross ownership restriction to withstand intermediate scrutiny under point four of *O'Brien*. Both cases involve challenges to the 1984 Cable Act's ban on telephone companies offering video programming in their service areas. In a case involving the Chesapeake and Potomac Telephone Company, the U.S. Court of Appeals for the Fourth Circuit found that "the FCC's reasoning does not indicate that attention was devoted to the possibility of other, less drastic regulatory schemes that might achieve the substantial government interests enunciated above."[89] Likewise, the Ninth Circuit found in *US West* that less restrictive means of promoting diversity could be found, and that a factual record had not been developed sufficiently to show that the ban on video service would advance diversity or competition in the cable industry.[90] The Supreme Court had been expected to view the matter in a similar light, but passage of the Telecommunications Act of 1996 (which repealed the telephone company restriction) precluded further judicial action.

News America Publishing, Inc. v. FCC

Newspaper/broadcast cross ownership cases are not the type to make headlines—except when they involve Rupert Murdoch. The media mogul's efforts to retain both a newspaper and television station in Boston ended up involving not only the FCC, but Congress and a U.S. court of appeals as well. The court never reached the constitutionality of the cross ownership ban itself but the case had First Amendment implications, largely unintended but nonetheless significant, that extended beyond Murdoch and persisted for almost a decade.

Murdoch's News America Publishing owned the NEW YORK POST and BOSTON HERALD. When Murdoch's Fox Television, Inc. acquired WNYW-TV in New York City and WXNE-TV in Boston, News America received temporary waivers to the newspaper/broadcast cross ownership rule from the FCC. The possibility existed that Murdoch would try to effect a "permanent" waiver by seeking a series of extensions of the temporary waivers. The Boston situation was reportedly of special concern to Sen. Edward M. Kennedy (D-Mass.).

Accordingly, in December 1987 Congress passed and the president signed a 1988 appropriations bill that included the following language inserted by Sen. Ernest F. Hollings (D-S.C.) at the behest of Sen. Kennedy:

> Provided, further, that none of the funds appropriated by this Act or any other Act may be used to repeal, to retroactively apply changes in, or to begin or continue a reexamination of the rules of the Federal Communications Commission with respect to the common ownership of a daily newspaper and a television station where the grade A contour of the television station encompasses the entire community in which the newspaper is published, or to extend the time period of current grants of temporary waivers to achieve compliance with such rules.[91]

News America applied for waiver extensions nonetheless and was turned down by the FCC in January 1988. The matter ended up in the U.S. Court of Appeals for the D.C. Circuit as a challenge to the First and Fifth Amendments (the equal protection mandate of the due process clause).[92] The court found that the last 18 words of the Hollings amendment targeted only one individual—Murdoch—since News America was the only entity holding any such temporary waivers.

The appeals court vacated the FCC's order denying the waiver request and remanded the case to the FCC for further consideration. The court cited a "violation of the free speech and equal protection guarantees of the First and Fifth Amendments," but noted also that the first part of the amendment (regarding repeal of the entire ban) was not ripe for review. The court did observe that "First Amendment values are implicated in the [waiver] process and require even-handed treatment of all applicants,"[93] but otherwise said nothing new or noteworthy regarding the First Amendment.

What makes the Murdoch case more than a curious footnote, however, is the fact that the language prohibiting repeal of the newspaper/broadcast ban reappeared in all subsequent appropriations bills and continuing resolutions until a budget was enacted on April 26, 1996. Thus, from 1988 through the first four months of 1996 there was no avenue for repeal of the newspaper/broadcast ban. The FCC's hands were tied by Congress; Congress itself missed the chance to mandate repeal in the Telecommunications Act of 1996; and there was no case in the courts reaching the question of repeal.

Thus, if one believes the newspaper/broadcast cross ownership rule is an unconstitutional suppression of free expression, the Hollings amendment proved to be an unintended case of "justice delayed, justice denied." The language aimed at Rupert Murdoch had a long-term effect on the newspaper and broadcasting industries (by delaying FCC review or repeal of the ban) that reached far beyond the Kennedy-Murdoch dispute. This amendment (which some have characterized as nothing more than a fit of senatorial pique over the Australian press lord) forestalled for years the easiest way of remedying this constitutional infirmity—a simple repeal of the rule by the FCC.

CHAPTER 5

Competition and Antitrust Concerns

The newspaper/broadcast cross ownership rule, like all other ownership rules, is couched in language that speaks of a dual purpose: creating viewpoint diversity and fostering economic competition. As we turn our attention from diversity and consider the FCC's interest in promoting a competitive marketplace, two aspects are obvious at the outset.

First, when the FCC talks about increasing competition, it really is talking about prohibiting excessive media concentration. Second, the FCC's concern over market concentration is not primarily an economic one, like that of the Federal Trade Commission, but is directly related to its desire for viewpoint diversity. The Commission believes that having fewer media owners in a given market results in fewer voices reaching the public, and that having more owners yields more voices.[94] Thus, even when we seem to be talking about economic competition, we are actually coming back to our initial discussion of viewpoint diversity.

This concern over concentration goes back to the earliest days of radio, when it was perceived that a large, established player like AT&T could monopolize both airwaves and editorial content if given the chance. As we noted in Chapter 2, this was a major reason the government felt compelled to adopt a regulatory scheme for broadcasting rather than allow private interests free rein. Paradoxically, this allocation plan also *reduced* the diversity that existed just prior to its implementation. So many broadcasters were vying for frequencies that signal overlap and interference had become a critical problem addressable only, it seemed, through government award of licenses to some and not others.[95]

The airwaves had become overcrowded with too many voices trying to be heard, and the government took it upon itself to pare down that overwhelming diversity to a level that could be accommodated by the technology of the day. "Unlimited diversity" thus served the public interest no better than, and in fact worse than, a monopoly; the former was a useless cacophony while the latter offered at least one voice. Therefore, the task of the Federal Radio Commission and later the FCC became one of manipulating market entry not only to prevent concentration but also to achieve maximum dispersion of ownership among the fixed number of station licenses it made available.[96]

Unfortunately, however, early ownership restrictions like the chain broadcasting and duopoly rules were better at preventing concentration than at promoting diversity. That is, they only enhanced diversity as a secondary effect of preventing concentration, rather than proactively creating diversity through other means. This shortcoming has been inherent in all subsequent ownership restrictions, including the newspaper/broadcast cross ownership rule. It's a classic case of trying to cut the existing pie into smaller pieces rather than baking a bigger pie.

Regulating competition

At the time it adopted the newspaper/broadcast ban, the Commission acted as if it were reacting to a situation that had sprung up without its knowledge or approval. This of course was not the case at all, because over the years the Commission had granted licenses to the scores of publishers who owned stations as of 1975. The FCC knew exactly to whom it was issuing licenses, and the extent of their publishing interests. In fact, in the early days of television the FCC not only allowed but actually *encouraged* newspaper publishers to apply for TV licenses because there was a shortage of qualified applicants. Newspaper owners, with their proven track record of providing information to the public, were considered highly desirable television licensees.[97] And as the Supreme Court has noted, in the ensuing years "the Commission has repeatedly renewed such licenses on findings that continuation of the service offered by the common owner would serve the public interest."[98] Thus it was no accident that by 1975 a substantial number of newspapers and broadcast outlets were commonly owned.[99]

The Commission acknowledged that it had sought out publishers in response to market conditions of the 1940s—a shortage of qualified TV applicants in the business community at large. In adopting the rule in 1975, the Commission made the same claim, that it was responding to market conditions (which now had changed to include *too many* publishers in broadcasting, in its view). In reality, however, the newspaper/broadcast ban was merely a further attempt to manipulate entry and thereby control competition within a closed regulatory framework. "Encouraging competition" had become a euphemism for "limiting market entry to non-publishers" and "creating the appearance of marketplace competition in a regulated industry."

FCC as antitrust cop? Factors such as company size and business practices are typically regulated by the U.S. Department of Justice and the Federal Trade Commission for purely economic reasons related to anticompetitive behavior. For example, the Justice Department may deny a proposed merger between two dominant companies in a market for fear the giant new entity would possess too much power to set prices and drive out smaller competitors.

In the broadcasting industry, such factors are also subject to review by the FCC through its licensing application and renewal process. The Commission's primary stated purpose is to enhance viewpoint diversity through ownership diversity, but it claims a secondary (or "correlative") authority on economic and antitrust grounds. In this way it mimics the actions of Justice and FTC, but in a manner more reminiscent of the proverbial horse walking backwards.

"Although the Commission is not empowered to enforce the antitrust laws, it may properly take cognizance of antitrust violations and antitrust policy in performing its public interest licensing function," the FCC said when it adopted the newspaper/broadcast ban.[100] Elaborating on this point in *RCA*, the Supreme Court had said in dictum:

> [I]n a given case the Commission might find that anti-trust considerations alone would keep the statutory standard from being met, as when the publisher of the sole newspaper in an area applies for a license for the only available radio and television facilities, which, if granted, would give him a monopoly of that area's major media of mass communication.[101]

It seems more likely in such a case, however, that the FCC would oppose the potential monopoly primarily on the grounds of viewpoint diversity. Indeed, the Commission explained the approach it took in fashioning the newspaper/broadcast ban as follows:

> [W]e have analyzed the basic media ownership questions in terms of this agency's primary concern—diversity in ownership as a means of enhancing diversity in programming service to the public—rather than in terms of a strictly antitrust approach....
>
> The distinction between our approach and the Justice Department's is best put this way. Justice and others applying traditional anti-trust criteria are primarily interested in preserving competition in advertising...and for their arguments they use analytic tools taken from economic studies of market share and the like. Conversely, the diversity approach would examine the number of voices available to the people of a given area.[102]

The only problem in tinkering with the economic dynamics of a market (*e.g.*, controlling entry and exit) to achieve a non-economic goal like viewpoint diversity is that such tinkering may have a serious negative impact on the economic viability of the market itself. It is quite possible to kill off the speakers in the process of enhancing their diversity.

The FCC seemed to come to this realization in the course of its rule-making on the newspaper/broadcast ban. A philosophical conflict had thus been raised: Was diversity such a preeminent goal that it should be pursued at all costs, including the economic disruption of the industry? The D.C. Circuit would later say that it should,[103] but the FCC found a way around the conundrum. The Commission invoked a still higher goal, its "ultimate goal" of serving the public interest. The public interest was well and necessarily served by diversity, the FCC said, but the public interest was served by other factors as well. These included market stability and continuity of ownership. "Promoting competition" by requiring divestiture of all newspaper/broadcast combinations might provide the "hoped for" diversity, but would disserve the public interest in some important ways: It could reduce local ownership, disrupt a station's continuity of operations and knowledge of the community, produce local economic dislocations, increase interest rates, and affect selling prices, the Commission acknowledged.[104]

The solution, then, was to create a balancing of competing goals under the broad umbrella of the "public interest." Diversity would be pursued, but not to the point of causing severe economic disruption to the industry. Therefore the newspaper/broadcast ban would be prospective in nature, prohibiting the formation of new combinations. Divestiture of existing combinations would not be required except in 16 "egregious" instances. (Of course "grandfathering" all but a handful of the existing combinations also had the practical benefit of neutralizing most of the likely opposition to the plan.)

What was amazing about the process was that the Commission sought to manipulate key market forces at the very heart of the industry's vitality for the sake of a goal (viewpoint diversity) that was merely speculative, and in the face of substantial evidence showing the plan to be ill advised.

The nature of competition today

Proponents of the newspaper/broadcast ban fear that new combinations would result in increased market concentration. This concern is based on the assumption that newspapers and broadcast outlets are interchangeable or substitutable forms of media. It is clear, however, that the two are not substitutes for each other, either in terms of the product characteristics they offer their audiences, or as a vehicle for advertisers. As such, there should be no fear that common ownership will result in a homogeneous product (including editorial voice), or that there will be any loss of benefits to either consumers or advertisers.

In the matter of product characteristics, for instance, broadcast outlets offer headlines and superficial coverage while newspapers offer detail and background; broadcasting is primarily an entertainment medium while newspapers are an information medium; newspapers provide a permanent record of events while broadcast outlets do not; people who rely primarily on television for their news do not necessarily subscribe to a newspaper; and the two media offer different forms of advertising.[105]

When it comes to advertising, newspapers offer mainly local advertising while television advertising is primarily national; local television ads lean heavily toward car dealers, while local newspaper advertising relies on department stores, supermarkets, car dealers, and real estate interests; there is no broadcast equivalent to newspapers' classified advertising; and there is no equivalent among newspapers to radio's highly segmented demographics according to station format.

Better quality. A number of studies at the time of the rulemaking found that television stations in newspaper/broadcast combinations actually provide a slightly higher quality of programming. Others found the influence of newspaper ownership to be negligible or inconclusive.

A statistical study by the FCC itself found that commonly owned stations "programmed more local news, and local non-entertainment programming, and more local programming generally, than independently owned stations."[106] Two Rand Corporation studies found "a lack of concrete evidence of harm from cross ownership." A performance ranking by a former FCC commissioner "rated newspaper owner licensees quite respectably compared to other individual and group stations."[107] And another statistical analysis found that newspaper ownership does not affect program diversity, profitability, revenues, time sales, audience size, or amounts of news, entertainment, feature films, or local programming.[108]

The economic advantage of cross ownership

In purely economic terms, media competition would be genuinely enhanced in a world without the newspaper/broadcast ban. This will be viewed as a provocative claim by proponents of regulation who fear the specter of gigantic media conglomerates gobbling up every outlet in sight. First, let us address that concern. The reality of today's media marketplace is that consolidation *has* taken place to varying degrees in certain segments of the market. That trend is likely to continue as media owners strive for economic efficiencies and economies of scale—there is no evidence whatsoever to suggest this is an attempt by a handful of media kingpins to monopolize the viewpoints reaching their audiences. Cable systems, for example, have undergone significant consolidation; newspaper ownership has been consolidated as well, and today there are 352 independently owned dailies with the rest being group owned or publicly traded. Yet there is no ban preventing the common ownership of newspapers and cable systems, and the lack of such a ban has not resulted in any discernible anticompetitive behavior or loss of viewpoint diversity.

On the broadcasting side, the lack of a newspaper/broadcast ban would not result in media conglomerates of unlimited size; on the contrary, the number of broadcast outlets per market and national TV audience percentage are clearly limited by the Telecommunications Act of 1996. (See Chapter 1.) Non-publishers, in fact, are already able to take advantage of the more competitive environment created by the Telecom Act, leaving newspaper publishers at a distinct competitive disadvantage.

Turn now to the issue of marginally profitable newspapers and broadcast outlets, for here is where repeal of the ban would yield real increases in competition. Absent the cross ownership ban, a marginal broadcast outlet (most likely a UHF television station or a smaller radio station) could be acquired by a profitable newspaper, or a failing newspaper could be bought by a profitable broadcast outlet. Resources from the profitable outlet could be used to upgrade the marginal outlet, thereby strengthening its competitive posture in the local market—or in many cases, no doubt, keeping it from going out of business altogether.

Perhaps the fate of the WASHINGTON STAR might have been different in the absence of the cross ownership ban. In 1975 the Commission granted a three-year temporary waiver to Joe L. Allbritton's Perpetual Corporation, allowing it to take control of the paper's parent company and its broadcast holdings. Perpetual was able to show the STAR was in danger of failing, which would have left the WASHINGTON POST with a virtual newspaper monopoly. The paper stayed afloat during that period of local cross ownership and was purchased in 1978 by Time Inc. But Time's interest waned in 1981 and the STAR folded, absent the waiver and without the prospect of a local station owner coming to the rescue.[109]

Increasingly, repeal of the ban would likely work to the benefit of struggling daily newspapers whose ranks have shrunk dramatically in recent decades. Just since the newspaper/broadcast ban was adopted in 1975, for example, the number of daily newspapers has declined 11 percent, from 1,756 to 1,556.[110]

Repealing the ban would also reduce the economic inefficiencies that occur when the Commission regulates an economic factor (market entry) to achieve a non-economic goal (viewpoint diversity). Consider a case in which the optimal buyer (in economic terms) for a particular outlet already owns an outlet in a different medium in that market. The Commission will not allow the purchase, thereby forcing the potential buyer to make another investment elsewhere that may be less than optimal. The outlet in question, meanwhile, may be bought by a less-than-optimal purchaser. There is no way to calculate the amount of resources that have been wasted through such inefficient allocation.

In addition to these economic benefits, cross ownership would actually promote diversity in cases where the only alternative is a newspaper going out of business or a broadcast outlet going silent. Keeping a media outlet alive helps preserve diversity, and the ban is clearly counterproductive when it forecloses a combination that could mean the survival of another voice.[111] Common ownership could also be beneficial in instances where survival is not at issue. As the FCC noted recently: "There may also be cases where cross ownership, while not necessary to the viability of one or both outlets, could lead to benefits such as increased dissemination of news and information in the relevant local market and have only a negligible effect on ownership diversity and competition."[112]

The risks of media concentration have been blown far out of proportion in relation to the benefits that would likely accrue to struggling newspapers and broadcast outlets. Repeal of the newspaper/broadcast ban would create the same competitive opportunities in local markets for these papers and outlets now being enjoyed by multiple station owners and by grandfathered newspaper/broadcast combinations.

A way to improve competition

Experience in the media industry teaches that there is one sure-fire way for government to improve competition: move from a regulatory model to a marketplace model. Creating a media environment in which competition can flourish invariably leads to a larger market and more competitors—and each new competitor is potentially another voice adding to viewpoint diversity. Repeal of the newspaper/broadcast ban would thus be consistent with a structural approach to creating a more competitive media landscape.

A few brief examples show the competitive benefits of a marketplace structure. For years the FCC sought to promote the development of broadcast television and specifically, as time went on, of UHF TV. One way the Commission went about this was to stifle the development of cable television, which it viewed as a threat to broadcasting.

UHF television continued to languish, however, even with passage of the All Channel Receiver Act in 1962. It was not until the Commission lifted cable TV restrictions in the late 1970s that UHF took off—because these stations were now being carried on rapidly spreading cable systems reaching far wider audiences.

Likewise, repeal of the financial interest and syndication rules in the early 1990s was directly responsible for the expansion of the Fox Network and the creation of two new broadcast networks—The WB and UPN. It is no coincidence that all three networks are affiliated with movie studios. The fin/syn rules, which were intended to promote diversity by prohibiting network ownership of programming, had the counterproductive effect of keeping studios from starting their own networks. The gains in program diversity stemming from the addition of three new networks are obvious.

The benefits of creating a competitive environment have not gone unnoticed even by the current FCC regime. Chairman Reed Hundt and FCC economist Greg Rosston observed in a 1995 paper:

> There are numerous examples of spectrum restrictions that have minimized competition and cost consumers.... An enterprising company called Microwave Communications Inc. petitioned the Commission to allow it to use its microwave assignments for more comprehensive services. After significant delay and much opposition from the incumbent, the Commission allowed this use. The result was the creation of long distance telephone competition courtesy of the company now known as MCI....[113]

A stated goal of the FCC's ownership rules is to increase diversity by encouraging competition. But competition cannot be imposed through regulation. A truly competitive and diverse media marketplace is achieved by allowing market forces to work. Repealing the newspaper/broadcast cross ownership rule will allow market forces to work in these segments, and is a necessary element in reaching the level of competition that yields genuine diversity.

CHAPTER 6

Conclusion: Why the Newspaper/Broadcast Cross Ownership Rule Should Be Repealed

> It may well be that some venerable FCC policies cannot withstand constitutional scrutiny in light of contemporary understanding of the First Amendment and the modern proliferation of broadcast outlets.
>
> — U.S. Court of Appeals for the District of Columbia[114]

When we analyze the newspaper/broadcast cross ownership rule according to any of the criteria we have used thus far we reach the same conclusion: The rule no longer serves a purpose (if it ever did) and should be repealed.

We can reach this conclusion by looking at any single factor: the dramatic changes in the media marketplace since the rule was adopted; the demise of scarcity in all forms—absolute numbers, economic, and speaker access; the First Amendment implications stemming from the absence of scarcity; the economic inefficiencies that result from manipulating competition to achieve a non-economic goal; deregulatory actions already undertaken by Congress and the FCC; the demonstrated benefits to consumers of a market-driven industry over a regulated industry; and the whole notion of government-imposed diversity. Taken together, these factors present an irrefutable case for repeal.

Market conditions have changed dramatically since the ban took effect in 1975. The newspaper/broadcast ban was adopted in response to the media market of the late 1960s and early '70s—a time when the newspaper industry was relatively robust, the "big three" networks ruled television, UHF TV was barely a force, and cable had yet to explode as the dominant distribution system. Other "new media" like DBS, "wireless cable," VCRs, and interactive services were years and even decades away from becoming household items.

A regulation adopted to respond to a market at a certain point in time should change when that market changes—especially when the media market has changed as dramatically and extensively as it has in the past three decades.

Media scarcity no longer exists, eliminating any need for the government to impose diversity. The newspaper/broadcast ban was based on the premise that viewpoint diversity is a desirable trait of the broadcast industry, and that government had to impose that diversity because broadcasting media were a scarce resource. Today, however, there is no scarcity whatsoever in the electronic media marketplace by any measure.

In absolute numbers, far more outlets exist today than in 1970, the year the ban was proposed. Television stations have jumped 80 percent, from 862 to 1,544; radio outlets have increased similarly from 6,995 to 12,134; and subscribers to basic cable service rose from 4.5 million to 62.1 million. Millions of viewers receive programming via direct broadcast satellite, "wireless cable," and other delivery systems that did not exist in 1970. Ironically, if any medium has become more scarce in numerical terms it is newspapers. The number of daily papers has declined since 1975 from 1,756 to 1,556.

It is time to put the confusion to rest that broadcast spectrum will be scarce as long as there are more would-be broadcasters than frequencies to go around. In economic terms, all resources that are not infinite are "scarce" in this way. By this criterion spectrum is no more scarce than any other economic good—even printing presses and ink. This "economic scarcity" is addressed by a lively secondary market in broadcast licenses which, by setting market prices, ensures that there is no shortage of licenses available to buyers willing to pay the price.

In addition, there is no longer any significant media scarcity in terms of speakers' access. According to the old argument, broadcast media were scarce because not every individual could own a station as a platform for his or her views. The explosion of cable, however, has made it possible for the average citizen to have access to cablecasting through a variety of local access, leased access, and PEG (public, educational, and governmental) channels. Moreover, everyone can now become an electronic publisher on the Internet through a personal home page or participation in thousands of user groups, bulletin boards, and chat rooms. Through the Internet, an individual potentially can reach far more people than by having a letter to the editor printed or even by starting a newspaper.

Given today's media abundance, the ban is of dubious constitutional validity. When the Supreme Court upheld the constitutionality of the newspaper/broadcast ban in 1978, it did so on the basis of the *Red Lion* scarcity rationale—that "spectrum scarcity" made broadcasting a unique situation that gave broadcasters fewer First Amendment rights. As a result, government regulation was subject to a relaxed level of scrutiny. Today, if the Court agreed that scarcity was no longer a significant problem it would have to give the ban at least the intermediate scrutiny of the *O'Brien* test. The ban would not survive such a challenge, because there is no factual record that it advances the government's interest in diversity, and it is not a narrowly tailored means, or even a reasonable means, of advancing that interest.

Furthermore, it is contrary to the First Amendment for the government to establish a privileged class of speakers (broadcasters who are not publishers, or vice versa) and thereby create a disadvantaged class having fewer speaking opportunities. Denying a media owner the right to speak in another local medium also deprives the listener of the right to receive that voice in that particular medium.

Repealing the ban would improve competition. One of the stated goals of the newspaper/broadcast ban is to improve competition, but the rule has become decidedly counterproductive in that regard.

Restrictions on most other types of cross ownership have been repealed, leaving the playing field tilted steeply against those who would like to own a newspaper and broadcast outlet in the same market. These individuals are now at a competitive disadvantage vis-à-vis common owners of newspapers and cable systems, television and radio stations, and television stations and cable systems—not to mention the owners of "grandfathered" newspaper/broadcast combinations.

In addition, the rule works against competition by making it impossible for a weak newspaper or broadcast outlet to benefit from the resources of a strong partner in the other medium. If the rule bars the only potential purchaser from buying a weak outlet, a newspaper may go out of business or a broadcast station may go off the air.

Furthermore, repealing the rule would reduce the economic inefficiencies that occur when the FCC regulates market factors to achieve a non-economic goal. The FCC controls market entry for the purpose of increasing viewpoint diversity (a non-economic goal). However, if the optimal buyer (in economic terms) for a given outlet already owns a different medium in that market, the FCC will block the purchase. The prospective buyer may then be forced to make a less-than-optimal investment elsewhere, while the outlet in question may be bought by a less-than-optimal purchaser. It is not hard to see how the newspaper/broadcast ban results in significant economic inefficiencies and misallocations of resources. Unfortunately, there is no way to calculate the extent to which resources have been misallocated or otherwise wasted because of the ban.

Finally, repealing the ban would move this segment of the media industry closer to a marketplace model where true competition—and a more efficient allocation of resources—can take place. The Department of Justice and the Federal Trade Commission would continue to oversee the media industry, as they do other industries, to guard against excessive economic concentration and anticompetitive practices.

The arguments outlined above weigh conclusively in favor of repealing the newspaper/broadcast ban. As a practical matter, however, we may be tilting at windmills if political sentiment is undauntedly opposed to change. Surprisingly, perhaps, that may not be the case. Over the last decade both Congress and the FCC have taken actions that indicate an awareness of the changing media environment and a willingness to move toward a more competitive model, especially where certain regulations have proved outmoded and counterproductive.

The FCC, for example, has taken the following steps:

- Declared in 1985 that scarcity no longer existed, and that "intrusion by government" was no longer warranted: "We believe that the interest of the public in viewpoint diversity is fully served by the multiplicity of voices in the marketplace today...."[115]
- Repealed the Fairness Doctrine in 1987, citing the "explosive growth" in media since *Red Lion*.
- Repealed the financial interest and syndication rules, saying they had become counterproductive to their goal of enhancing diversity in programming.
- Repealed the prime time access rule because market growth had made government intervention unnecessary.
- Relaxed program log and other administrative requirements, citing the prospect of an even more competitive environment.
- Eased the "one-to-a-market" rule to allow common ownership of a television station, AM, and FM radio station in the same market.
- Progressively raised the cap on the number of television and radio stations one entity could own nationally.

Congress, meanwhile, was moving in a similar direction in many regards. Lawmakers did the following:

- Passed the Telecommunications Act of 1996 that removed the cap on the number of television and radio stations one entity could own nationally.
- Established generous caps on the number of radio stations one entity could own in a market.
- Repealed the statutory ban on cable/broadcast cross ownership, and directed the FCC to repeal its cable/network cross ownership rule.

- Repealed the statutory ban on telephone companies competing with cable operators.
- Initially included repeal of the newspaper/broadcast ban as a part of that legislative package, but dropped it in the course of negotiations.
- Mandated biennial review by the FCC of all its ownership regulations, including the newspaper/broadcast ban.
- In a separate action, removed the funding restriction in FCC appropriations legislation that had prohibited the Commission, since 1988, from reviewing or repealing the newspaper/broadcast ban.

Taken together, these actions by both the Commission and Congress would seem to indicate a philosophical predisposition toward making the media industry more competitive by removing unnecessary regulations. Unfortunately, that sentiment has not as yet moved either body to repeal the newspaper/broadcast rule. The fact that its repeal was dropped from the telecom bill indicates some obvious opposition among lawmakers. However, if the newspaper/broadcast ban was merely horse traded for some other provision (say, for instance, a 35-percent cap on national audience), the effect has been to leave prospective owners of such combinations at a competitive disadvantage for no real reason.

The situation may be more understandable at the Commission, given the fact that the FCC was prohibited by Congress, until April 1996, from repealing the ban. But neither the lifting of that prohibition nor the sweeping nature of the Telecom Act itself gave the FCC enough of a cue to move forward toward repeal. Instead, the Commission has been content to initiate a rather tepid rulemaking to allow more newspaper/radio waivers that fails to address the newspaper/television issue at all.

We are left wondering why Congress and the Commission have both left this one cross ownership rule as a sort of vestigial reminder of the 1970s. The rule was adopted without evidence that it was responding to any documented harm (indeed, the Commission admitted there was no evidence of abuse by combination owners at the time) and its intended benefits were speculative at best. The rule may well have had more to do with the anti-media political climate of the day (owing, for example, to the Vietnam War and Watergate) than with its stated purposes.

We can ascertain no good reason for the rule's continued existence today. It does appear, however, that the stage is now set—and ample precedent exists—should either body decide to repeal the newspaper/broadcast ban. Repeal is long overdue and should be undertaken at once.

* * * *

In closing, two other points demand attention. Both affect the newspaper/broadcast ban directly, but go far beyond that particular rule. And if these issues are too far-reaching for the scope of this discussion, perhaps they will provide grist for debate in other venues at other times.

The first deals with the concept of competition versus regulation. Experience in non-regulated segments of the media shows that competition ultimately serves the public interest far better than regulation by generating media growth, technological innovation, higher quality programming, more efficient allocation of resources, and greater diversity. By contrast, it is hard to imagine that this country would be the world leader in computer technology if that industry had been hobbled by government regulations that retarded innovation and imposed economic burdens on computer companies under the guise of "serving the public interest."

Despite taking the pro-competition actions cited above, however, neither Congress nor the FCC seems ready to embrace the idea of a fully competitive media industry that can function with no more government oversight (*i.e.*, FTC, Justice Dept.) than other industries. A number of recent actions, such as the Communications Decency Act and the V-chip mandate, suggest the pendulum may in fact be swinging back toward regulation. And the current Commission is certainly not known as a deregulatory regime in the manner of the Reagan and Bush commissions. The realities of the marketplace and the needs of consumers, however, dictate that the government serve the public interest by encouraging a competitive media industry. Stifling media development with burdensome regulation is not in the public interest.

The second point deals with the concept of diversity. Perhaps it is time for the courts to rethink the whole idea of the diversity principle as a tenet of First Amendment jurisprudence. The First Amendment was envisioned, first and foremost, as a means of protecting speech from government censorship. Certainly the value of speech to the listener is an important consideration in a democracy—but it remains a pleasant by-product of guaranteeing the rights of speakers. Especially in the broadcast realm, however, this relationship has been turned on its head and always justified because of the "unique situation" of spectrum scarcity. Guaranteeing a diverse batch of viewpoints for the benefit of the listener has become more important than guaranteeing the right of speakers to speak.

Adding insult to this injury is the idea of government-imposed diversity. This necessarily means stifling one voice so that another can be heard. It is hard to imagine how silencing certain speakers can be done for the purpose of encouraging free speech, yet this is what the FCC and the courts have asked us to believe. Perhaps when Congress, the courts, and the FCC all acknowledge that scarcity is no longer an issue and start acting accordingly, the principle of diversity can be returned to its proper place as secondary to the rights of speakers. Ultimately, diversity will be achieved not by government regulation of who may speak and who may not, but by guaranteeing a voice to all comers, to the widest possible array of speakers.

In the short term, the newspaper/broadcast cross ownership rule should be repealed. We have outlined the reasons for repeal, and they are compelling. The *effects* of repeal would be equally compelling. Removal of this structural barrier would create a level playing field and could be expected to keep some struggling media voices in business. Based on the performance of grandfathered combinations, we would expect new combinations to offer programming that was frequently of higher-than-average quality—the real measure of serving the public interest. And repeal of the ban would certainly have a salutary effect on the First Amendment rights of publishers and broadcasters as speakers.

In the bigger picture, moreover, repeal of the newspaper/broadcast ban would be a small step toward a more competitive media industry better able to meet the needs of today's consumer/citizen. And such a pro-First Amendment action might play a small role in putting the diversity principle in a more appropriate perspective in today's marketplace of media abundance. As the Commission itself said in a particularly prescient moment: "[I]t is through the protection of the rights of *speakers* that the interest of society as a whole will best be protected."[116]

Notes

Chapter 1

[1] *FCC Multiple Ownership Rule*, 47 C.F.R. Section 73.3555(c) (1993). The rule states:

> No license for an AM, FM, or TV broadcast station shall be granted to any party (including all parties under common control) if such party directly or indirectly owns, operates, or controls a daily newspaper and the grant of such license will result in:
>
> (1) The predicted or measured 2mV/m contour for an AM station, computed in accordance with Section 73.183 or Section 73.186, encompassing the entire community in which such newspaper is published; or
>
> (2) The predicted 1mV/m contour for an FM station, computed in accordance with Section 73.313, encompassing the entire community in which such newspaper is published; or
>
> (3) The Grade A contour for a TV station, computed in accordance with Section 73.684, encompassing the entire community in which such newspaper is published.

Congress included language aimed at Rupert Murdoch in the 1988 appropriations bill that prohibited the FCC from reviewing or repealing the newspaper/broadcast ban. That language persisted until 1994, when

Congress allowed the Commission to consider a liberalized waiver policy for newspaper/radio combinations. The language did not disappear entirely until the budget bill of April 1996. Meanwhile, in the Telecommunications Act passed in February 1996, Congress directed the FCC to conduct a biennial review of all its ownership rules, including the newspaper/broadcast ban.

[2] Telecommunications Act of 1996, Pub. L. No. 104-104, 110 Stat. 56 (1996). A helpful publication is Charles D. Ferris, Frank W. Lloyd, and Howard J. Symons, *Guidebook to the Telecommunications Act of 1996* (New York: Matthew Bender & Co., Inc., 1996).

[3] *Amendment of Sections 73.35, 73.240 and 73.636 of the Commission's Rules Relating to Multiple Ownership of Standard, FM and Television Broadcast Stations, First Report and Order,* 22 F.C.C.2d 306 (1970) ("1970 First Report and Order").

[4] *Amendment of Sections 73.35, 73.240 and 73.636 of the Commission's Rules Relating to Multiple Ownership of Standard, FM and Television Broadcast Stations, Further Notice of Proposed Rulemaking*, 22 F.C.C.2d 339, 340 (1970) (citation omitted) ("1970 Further Notice").

[5] *Id.* at 344 (citation omitted).

[6] *Id.*

[7] *Amendment of Sections 73.34, 73.240 and 73.636 of the Commission's Rules Relating to Multiple Ownership of Standard, FM and Television Broadcast Stations, Second Report and Order*, 50 F.C.C.2d 1046, 1048 (1975) ("1975 Second Report and Order").

[8] *Id.* at paras. 101-107, 112, 117.

[9] *Id.* at para. 119.

[10] *Id.* at paras. 108, 109. The 1975 Second Report and Order at para. 49 noted 94 newspaper/broadcast combinations "at the time the proceeding began" (1970), but at para. 112, n.29 noted 96 combinations in 1970 and 94 in 1971.

[11] *Amendment of Section 73.3555 of the Commission's Rules, the Broadcast Multiple Ownership Rules, First Report and Order*, 4 FCC Rcd. 1723 (adopted Oct. 27, 1988) ("1988 First Report and Order").

[12] *Id.*

[13] *Id.*

[14] *Amendment of Section 73.3555 of the Commission's Rules, the Broadcast Multiple Ownership Rules, Second Report and Order*, 4 FCC Rcd. 1741 (adopted Dec. 12, 1988) ("1988 Second Report and Order").

[15] *Id.* at para. 1.

[16] *Id.*

[17] *Id.* at para. 4.

[18] *Id.* at para. 2.

[19] Telecommunications Act of 1996, Pub. L. No. 104-104, Section 202, 110 Stat. 56 (1996). The national ownership caps removed by Congress had been relaxed progressively over the years by the FCC. A series of actions in the 1940s resulted in a limit of 7 AM, 6 FM, and 5 TV outlets by 1946. The limit was raised to 7 AM, 7 FM, and 7 TV (5 UHF) in 1953; 12 AM, 12 FM, and 12 TV in 1984; 18 AM and 18 FM in 1992, rising to 20 AM and 20 FM two years hence; and 14 TV stations in 1993, provided two or more were minority controlled (otherwise a limit of 12 non-minority controlled TV stations).

[20] *See, e.g.,* 141 Cong. Rec. E-1571 (Aug. 1, 1995) (Rep. Edward J. Markey (D-Mass.) discussing H.R. 1555).

[21] *Newspaper/Radio Cross-Ownership Waiver Policy, Notice of Inquiry, MM Docket No. 96-197*, FCC 96-381 (Sept. 17, 1996) ("1996 Notice of Inquiry").

[22] H.R. Rep. No. 103-293, 103rd Cong. 1st Sess. at 40, quoted in 1996 Notice of Inquiry, *supra* at 5.

[23] 1988 Second Report and Order, *supra* note 14 at para. 76.

[24] *See, e.g., Comments of Knight-Ridder, Inc. in MM Docket No. 96-197* (Feb. 7, 1997) at 5: "Without explaining why, the Commission's recent Notice of Inquiry cuts the rule down the middle and seeks comment only with respect to radio-newspaper combinations. Such an artificial dichotomy ignores the background and thrust of the rule." *See also, e.g., Comments of Freedom of Expression Foundation, Inc.* (FCC preferably should repeal entire rule).

[25] 1996 Notice of Inquiry, *supra* note 21 at 6.

Chapter 2

[26] Craig R. Smith, ed., *The Diversity Principle: Friend or Foe of the First Amendment?* (Washington, D.C.: The Media Institute, 1989) at 1.

[27] *Associated Press v. United States*, 326 U.S. 1, 20 (1945).

[28] *New York Times Co. v. Sullivan*, 376 U.S. 254, 270 (1964).

[29] *Red Lion Broadcasting Co. v. FCC*, 395 U.S. 367, 390 (1969).

[30] Ithiel de Sola Pool, *Technologies of Freedom* (Cambridge, Mass.: Harvard University Press, 1983) at 136-37.

[31] *Great Lakes Broadcasting Co.*, 3 F.R.C. Ann. Rep. 32, 33-35 (1929), quoted in FCC, *Public Service Responsibility of Broadcast Licensees* (Washington, D.C.: Government Printing Office, 1946) at 10. This content-specific approach clearly violated the intent of the "public interest" standard according to its legislative history. (*See, e.g.*, debate between Reps. LaGuardia and White on House floor in 1927.)

[32] *Report on Editorializing by Broadcast Licensees*, 13 F.C.C. 1246, 1249 (1949) ("1949 Report on Editorializing"). In 1941 the Commission ruled in *Mayflower Broadcasting* that the license of the Yankee Network would be renewed provided the licensee agreed not to editorialize. *Mayflower Broadcasting Corp.*, 8 F.C.C. 333 (1941). This blatant intrusion on First Amendment rights was remedied to a degree by the 1949 Report on Editorializing. The report allowed broadcasters to editorialize but also imposed the Fairness Doctrine, which required coverage of controversial issues of public importance and the presentation of contrasting viewpoints on those issues.

[33] 1970 Further Notice, *supra* note 4 at 344.

[34] *Id.*

[35] 1975 Second Report and Order, *supra* note 7 at para. 14.

[36] *Id.* at para. 10. The order also cited *Citizens Committee To Save WEFM v. FCC*, 506 F.2d 246, 268 (D.C. Cir. 1974) (Bazelon, C.J., concurring); *FCC v. Pottsville Broadcasting Co.*, 309 U.S. 134, 137 (1940); *FCC v. Sanders Bros. Radio Station*, 309 U.S. 470, 474-76 (1940); and *Mt. Mansfield TV Inc. v. FCC*, 442 F.2d 470 (2nd Cir. 1971).

[37] 1949 Report on Editorializing, *supra* note 32 at 1249.

[38] 1996 Notice of Inquiry, *supra* note 21 at 2.

[39] 1975 Second Report and Order, *supra* note 7 at para. 14.

[40] *Id.* at para. 11.

[41] By the time the Commission relaxed the radio/television cross ownership ban in 1988, it had acknowledged that common ownership does not imply a common voice: "[T]he joint ownership of two or more media outlets in the same market does not necessarily lead to a commonality of viewpoints by those outlets." 1988 Second Report and Order, *supra* note 14 at 1744.

[42] *Red Lion v. FCC*, 395 U.S. at 390.

[43] *Id.* at 389.

[44] *The Handling of Public Issues Under the Fairness Doctrine and the Public Interest Standards of the Communications Act*, 48 F.C.C.2d 1, 17 (1974) ("1974 Fairness Report").

[45] Lorna H. Veraldi suggests another impetus for the rule, that politicians were coming to fear the power of an ever larger and more contentious press: "The push for cross ownership rules, at least in part, may have been motivated by a desire to limit the power of an adversarial press.... During the 1960s, both ends of the political spectrum appeared to declare war on some nebulous monolith called 'big media.' The FCC's cross ownership rules arose as much from popular presumptions about the influence of 'media barons' as from any convincing evidence of abuse." Lorna H. Veraldi, *Carpooling on the Information Superhighway: The Case for Newspaper-Television Cross Ownership*, 8 ST. THOMAS L. REV. 349, 354 (Winter 1996) (citations omitted).

Chapter 3

[46] 1970 figure from *Amendment of Syndication and Financial Interest Rules, Tentative Decision and Request for Further Comments in BC Docket No. 82-345*, FCC 83-377, 48 Fed. Reg. 38,020 (Aug. 4, 1983) ("Tentative Decision"). 1997 number from BROADCASTING & CABLE, March 31, 1997 at 36.

[47] 1970 numbers from Tentative Decision, *supra*. 1997 numbers from *Broadcasting & Cable Yearbook 1997* (New Providence, N.J.: R.R. Bowker, 1997) at xxi.

[48] FCC, *Broadcast Station Totals as of May 31, 1996*, Mimeo No. 63298 (news release), June 6, 1996.

[49] 1970 number from Tentative Decision, *supra* note 46. 1997 number from *Broadcasting & Cable Yearbook 1997*, *supra* note 47.

[50] 1970 numbers from Tentative Decision, supra note 46. 1997 numbers from *Broadcasting & Cable Yearbook 1997*, *supra* note 47.

[51] Steve Sternberg, *Is Everything Nielsen's Fault?* INSIDE MEDIA, June 26, 1996 at 38.

[52] 1970 numbers from Tentative Decision, *supra* note 46. 1997 numbers from *Broadcasting & Cable Yearbook 1997*, *supra* note 47; and *Annual Assessment of the Status of Competition in the Market for the Delivery of Video Programming, Third Annual Report (Part 1),* FCC 96-496, 1997 Lexis 151, 5 Comm. Reg. (P.&F.) 1164 (Dec. 26, 1996) ("FCC Competition Report") at paras. 13-17.

[53] FCC Competition Report, *supra* at para. 4 (DBS), para. 53 (MMDS), para. 81 (SMATV).

[54] *Inquiry into Section 73.1910 of the Commission's Rules and Regulations Concerning the General Fairness Doctrine Obligations of Broadcast Licensees*, 102 F.C.C.2d 145, 147 (1985) ("1985 Fairness Report").

[55] *Id.* at 148.

[56] *Inquiry into Section 73.1910 of the Commission's Rules and Regulations Concerning Alternatives to the General Fairness Doctrine Obligations of Broadcast Licensees*, 2 FCC Rcd. 17 5272 (1987). In 1989 the D.C. Circuit upheld the Commission's decision to repeal the Fairness Doctrine: "We conclude that the FCC's decision that the fairness doctrine no longer served the public interest was neither arbitrary, capricious nor an abuse of discretion.... Accordingly we uphold the Commission without reaching the constitutional issues." *Syracuse Peace Council v. FCC*, 867 F.2d 654, 669 (D.C. Cir. 1989).

[57] *See Review of the Prime Time Access Rule, Section 73.658(k) of the Commission's Rules, Report and Order*, 11 FCC Rcd. 546, 547 (1995) ("PTAR Report and Order").

[58] *See Evaluation of the Syndication and Financial Interest Rules, Second Report and Order*, 8 FCC Rcd. 3282 (1993) ("Fin/Syn Second Report and Order"*), recon. granted in part, Memorandum Opinion and Order,* 8

FCC Rcd. 8270 (1993), *aff'd Capital Cities/ABC, Inc. v. FCC*, 29 F.3d 309 (7th Cir. 1994).

[59] PTAR Report and Order, *supra* note 57 at para. 20.

[60] Fin/Syn Second Report and Order, *supra* note 58 at para. 12. For a fuller discussion of the counterproductive nature of the fin/syn rules, see Richard T. Kaplar, *Prime Time for Repeal: The Financial Interest and Syndication Rules* (Washington, D.C.: The Media Institute, 1990).

[61] *Revision of Programming and Commercialization Policies, Ascertainment Requirements, and Program Log Requirements for Commercial Television Stations*, 98 F.C.C.2d 1075 (1994) at paras. 20-21. The rapid growth in radio had prompted the Commission to undertake a similar deregulation of certain requirements for that industry in 1981: "Policies that may have been necessary in the early days of radio may not be necessary in an environment where thousands of licensees offer diverse sorts of programming and appeal to all manner of segmented audiences." *Report and Order Adopted To Deregulate Commercial Broadcast Radio in the Areas of Nonentertainment Programming, Ascertainment, Commercialization, and Program Logs*, 84 F.C.C.2d 968 (1981) at paras. 2-3.

[62] *Red Lion v. FCC*, 395 U.S. at 393.

[63] *CBS, Inc. v. Democratic National Comm.*, 412 U.S. 94, 102 (1973).

[64] *FCC v. League of Women Voters of Calif.*, 468 U.S. 364, 376-77 (1984). Indeed, the Court has been reluctant to abandon its long-standing reliance on the scarcity rationale. Robert M. O'Neil notes that "scarcity has somehow persisted as a premise, or at least a pivotal assumption," and that "*Red Lion* has proved remarkably durable, given the frailty of its legal premises and the massive changes that have occurred in the electronic media." He is hopeful, however, that "change may now be in prospect, and for reasons the courts have just begun to appreciate." See Robert M. O'Neil, "Dead or Alive: How Long Will the Red Lion Specter Haunt Free Speech and Broadcasting?" in Robert Corn-Revere, ed., *Rationales & Rationalizations: Regulating the Electronic Media* (Washington, D.C.: The Media Institute, 1997) at 19-41.

[65] 1974 Fairness Report, *supra* note 44 at 4, n.4. D.C. Circuit Judge Starr referred to this as "allocational scarcity." *Syracuse Peace Council v. FCC*, 867 F.2d 654, 682 (1989) (Starr, J., concurring).

[66] *Telecommunications Research and Action Center v. FCC*, 801 F.2d 501, 508 (D.C. Cir. 1986), *cert. denied*, 482 U.S. 919 (1987).

[67] In the first three months of 1997 alone, radio and television stations changed hands in 265 transactions valued at $5.42 billion. BROADCASTING & CABLE, March 31, 1997 at 37.

[68] *Radio-Television News Directors Ass'n v. United States*, 400 F.2d 1002, 1019 (7th Cir. 1968), citing U.S. Bureau of the Census, *Statistical Abstract of the United States: 1967*, nos. 737, 746 (88th ed.).

[69] A local franchising authority can require a cable operator to provide "adequate" channel capacity for "PEG" use under the 1984 and 1992 Cable Acts. The acts also mandate that a cable operator set aside a proportional number of channels for leased commercial use by outsiders. 47 U.S.C. Sections 531, 532, 541. These provisions were held to be constitutional in *Time Warner Entertainment Co. v. FCC*, 93 F.3d 957, 967-73 (D.C. Cir. 1996) (*per curiam*).

[70] 1996 Notice of Inquiry, *supra* note 21 at 7.

Chapter 4

[71] *FCC v. National Citizens Comm. for Broadcasting*, 436 U.S. 775 (1978).

[72] *Id.* at 799.

[73] *Id.*

[74] *Id.* at 800, quoting *Red Lion v. FCC*, 395 U.S. at 389, quoting *NBC v. United States*, 319 U.S. at 227. In a further Orwellian twist, the Court said the rule's "purpose and effect is to promote free speech, not to restrict it." *Id.* at 801. For a discussion of how the FCC relies on euphemism as a regulatory tool, see Robert Corn-Revere, "'Voluntary' Self-Regulation and the Triumph of Euphemism," in Robert Corn-Revere, ed., *Rationales & Rationalizations: Regulating the Electronic Media* (Washington, D.C.: The Media Institute, 1997) at 183-214.

[75] *Id.* at 800-02. Another First Amendment argument contends that the newspaper/broadcast ban amounts to a prior restraint on speech. "Since a waiver may be granted in certain circumstances, a newspaper or broadcast proprietor may petition the Commission to grant a license despite its cross ownership status. The waiver request procedure may be analogized to a prior restraint circumstance, in which a speaker first must obtain city approval before printing a newspaper." Karen A. Hoffman, *Newspaper-Broadcast Cross Ownership Policy: A New Standard From Across the*

Border, 23 CASE W. RES. J. INT'L L. 333, 351 (Spring 1991) (citation omitted).

[76] *Id.* at 802.

[77] *Turner Broadcasting System, Inc. v. FCC*, 512 U.S. 622, 637 (1994).

[78] *FCC v. National Citizens Comm.*, 436 U.S. at 801.

[79] *United States v. O'Brien*, 391 U.S. 367, 377 (1968).

[80] *FCC v. National Citizens Comm.*, 436 U.S. at 793-94, *citing United States v. Storer Broadcasting Co.*, 351 U.S. 192 (1956); and *NBC v. United States*, 319 U.S. 190 (1943). "This Court has specifically upheld this rule-making authority in the context of regulations based on the Commission's policy of promoting diversification of ownership." *Id.* at 794.

[81] *Turner Broadcasting v. FCC*, 512 U.S. at 664.

[82] *Id. See also 44 Liquormart, Inc. v. Rhode Island*, 116 S. Ct. 1495 (1996) (merely "rational" or "reasonable" judgment of regulators absent an evidentiary record not entitled to judicial deference).

[83] 1970 Further Notice, *supra* note 4 at 344, n.6.

[84] 1975 Second Report and Order, *supra* note 7 at paras. 112, n.29; 119.

[85] *FCC v. National Citizens Comm.*, 436 U.S. at 796, 797.

[86] *Buckley v. Valeo*, 424 U.S. 1, 48-49 (1976).

[87] *See* Thomas W. Hazlett, "Market Failure as a Justification To Regulate Broadcast Communications," in Robert Corn-Revere, ed., *Rationales & Rationalizations: Regulating the Electronic Media* (Washington, D.C.: The Media Institute, 1997) at 166-71. See also Richard T. Kaplar and Patrick D. Maines, *The Government Factor: Undermining Journalistic Ethics in the Information Age* (Washington, D.C.: Cato Institute, 1995) at 35-47.

[88] *Complaint of Syracuse Peace Council Against Television Station WTVH*, 2 FCC Rcd. 5043 (1987) at para. 60.

[89] *Chesapeake and Potomac Telephone Co. v. United States*, 42 F.3d 181 (4th Cir. 1994), *cert. granted,* 115 S. Ct. 2608 (June 26, 1995), *vacated,* 116 S. Ct. 1036 (Feb. 27, 1996).

[90] *US West, Inc. v. United States*, 48 F.3d 1092 (9th Cir. 1995), *cert. granted, vacated,* 116 S. Ct. 1037 (March 4, 1996).

But on March 31, 1997, the Supreme Court upheld for the second time (and by the same narrow 5-4 margin) a lower court ruling that "must-carry" rules requiring cable operators to carry local broadcast signals are content-neutral restrictions that withstand the intermediate scrutiny of *O'Brien. Turner Broadcasting System, Inc. v. FCC*, No. 95-992 (S. Ct. March 31, 1997) ("*Turner II*"). In this second decision the principal opinion addressed only two remaining questions: (1) "not whether Congress was correct as an objective matter, but whether the legislative conclusion was reasonable and supported by substantial evidence" (it was, the Court found); and (2) whether the must-carry rules "burden substantially more speech than is necessary to further the governmental interests they promote" (they don't, the Court said). Justices O'Connor, Scalia, Thomas, and Ginsburg thought the rules content-specific and thus subject to strict scrutiny; their dissent summed up the shortcomings of the principal opinion as follows:

> [T]he Court ignores the main justification of the statute urged by appellees and subjects restrictions on expressive activity to an inappropriately lenient level of scrutiny [*O'Brien*]. The principal opinion then misapplies the analytic framework it chooses, exhibiting an extraordinary and unwarranted deference for congressional judgments, a profound fear of delving into complex economic matters, and a willingness to substitute untested assumptions for evidence." *Id.*, slip op. at 31 (O'Connor, J., et al., dissenting).

Even Justice Breyer, who concurred with the principal opinion's diversity argument (but not its anticompetitive rationale), noted that must-carry "extracts a serious First Amendment price.... This 'price' amounts to a 'suppression of speech.'" *Id.*, slip op. at 2 (Breyer, J., concurring in part). Nothing in *Turner II* suggests the newspaper/broadcast ban would withstand intermediate scrutiny under *O'Brien.*

[91] Pub. L. No. 100-202, 101 Stat. 1329 (1987); Making Further Continuing Appropriations for the Fiscal Year Ending September 30, 1988, H.R. Rep. No. 100-498, 100th Cong. 1st Sess. (1987) at 34. In the fall of 1987 the Freedom of Expression Foundation had filed a petition at the FCC seeking revision or repeal of the newspaper/broadcast ban—a factor cited by News America in its waiver request. The Commission dismissed the FOEF petition in 1991, however, citing the Hollings amendment that barred it from reviewing the cross ownership ban.

[92] *News America Publishing, Inc. v. FCC*, 844 F.2d 800 (1988).

[93] *Id.* at 815. Murdoch eventually sold both newspapers, mooting his First

Amendment claim. In an ironic development, however, the FCC granted him a *permanent* waiver to reacquire the NEW YORK POST, which otherwise was poised to go out of business. Thus, Murdoch came to hold one of only two permanent newspaper/broadcast waivers ever granted by the Commission. (The other was granted to Field Communications Corp. in Chicago, which reacquired a station it had originally owned under the grandfather clause. *Field Communications Corp.*, 65 F.C.C.2d 959 (1977).)

Chapter 5

[94] In adopting the rules in 1975 the Commission stated that "requiring competition in the market place of ideas is, in theory, the best way to assure a multiplicity of voices." 1975 Second Report and Order, *supra* note 7 at para. 11. In reality, however, the best way has proved to be allowing competition to develop freely, which has provided far more viewpoint diversity than "required competition" ever could.

[95] This is the traditional view of broadcast history. *See, e.g.*, FCC Office of Network Study, *Second Interim Report on Television Network Procurement* (1965). "With everybody on the air, nobody could be heard." *Id.* at 66. A contrary view is offered by Thomas W. Hazlett, who notes that interference had been a relatively minor problem regulated by the Commerce Department, relying on the "right of user" tradition in common law. "There then occurred what was labeled 'the period of the breakdown of the law.' Secretary of Commerce Herbert Hoover stopped enforcing radio rights in a discrete policy statement issued on July 9, 1926. It was clearly understood that this would create some confusion over interference parameters...but was Hoover's strategic ploy to build demand for licensing legislation which had stalled for years. The ploy worked, as the Radio Act was enacted Feb. 23, 1927. As the phrase suggests, however, order had reigned prior to the 'breakdown' of property rights." Hazlett, "Market Failure as a Justification To Regulate Broadcast Communications," *supra* note 87 at 162, n.20.

[96] Regardless of the magnitude of the interference problem, or the desire for ownership dispersion, there can be no doubt that keeping ultimate control of the airwaves in political hands was never far from the minds of lawmakers grappling with the structure of the nascent radio industry.

[97] In 1948, 48 percent of television stations were owned by newspapers; by the time the cross ownership ban was adopted in 1975, the percentage had shrunk to 10.4 percent. 1975 Second Report and Order, *supra* note 7 at para. 112, n.29. Newspaper publishers whose editorial viewpoints were

politically friendly were especially prized as potential television licensees, according to some observers at the time.

[98] *FCC v. National Citizens Committee*, 436 U.S. at 783.

[99] The Commission cited 79 television stations "owned partly or wholly in common with daily newspapers published in the same locality" as of July 1974, and the same number "at present" (January 1975). This was part of a downward trend: 96 newspaper/television combinations in 1970; 94 in 1971; and 83 in April 1974. 1975 Second Report and Order, *supra* note 7 at para. 112, n.29.

[100] *Id.* at para. 11.

[101] *United States v. RCA*, 358 U.S. 334, 351-52 (1959).

[102] 1975 Second Report and Order, *supra* note 7 at paras. 11, 12.

[103] *National Citizens Comm. for Broadcasting v. FCC*, 555 F.2d 938 (D.C. Cir. 1977), *aff'd in part, rev'd in part sub nom. FCC v. National Citizens Comm. for Broadcasting*, 436 U.S. 775. The D.C. Circuit found it logically inconsistent to require divestiture in certain but not all cases, and directed the Commission to adopt a rule requiring mandatory divestiture of all cross owned combinations. The Supreme Court reversed that directive.

[104] 1975 Second Report and Order, *supra* note 7 at para. 108.

[105] These and other characteristics are cited in the 1975 Second Report and Order, *supra* note 7 at para. 68.

[106] *Staff Study of 1973 Television Station Annual Programming Reports*, Appendix C, 1975 Second Report and Order, *supra* note 7.

[107] Statement of Commissioner Benjamin L. Hooks (concurring in part, dissenting in part), 1975 Second Report and Order, *supra* note 7 at 1109, n.1, n.2.

[108] Statement of Commissioner Glen O. Robinson (concurring in part, dissenting in part), *Id.* at 1121, n.18.

[109] *Crosby N. Boyd*, 57 F.C.C.2d 475, 484 (1975); *Evening Star Broadcasting Co.*, 68 F.C.C.2d 129 (1978).

[110] 1996 Notice of Inquiry, *supra* note 21 at 7. Seventeen newspapers now publish under joint operating agreements, a limited antitrust exemption enacted by Congress in 1970 that allows a struggling newspaper to share

production facilities with a competitor.

[111]This was the primary reason the FCC granted a permanent waiver to Rupert Murdoch for common ownership of the NEW YORK POST and WNYW-TV. "The Commission believed that...Murdoch's reacquisition of the Post might be pivotal to the paper's continued survival.... [F]ailure to grant the waiver would threaten the existence of an established media outlet...." *Id.* at 4.

In *Turner II*, Justice Breyer's swing vote upholding the must-carry rules was based on just such a diversity argument—that must-carry amounted to a form of economic subsidy which, by "guaranteeing the over-the-air stations...extra dollars," allowed them to stay on the air, thereby adding to the diversity of viewpoints reaching non-cable households. *Turner Broadcasting v. FCC*, *supra* note 90, slip op. at 1-2 (Breyer, J., concurring in part).

[112]1996 Notice of Inquiry, *supra* note 21 at 7 (citation omitted).

[113]Reed E. Hundt and Gregory L. Rosston, *Spectrum Flexibility Will Promote Competition and the Public Interest*, IEEE COMMUNICATIONS MAGAZINE, December 1995 at 41.

Chapter 6

[114]*Banzhaf v. FCC*, 405 F.2d 1082, 1100 (D.C. Cir. 1968), *cert. denied sub nom. Tobacco Institute v. FCC*, 396 U.S. 842 (1969). In the context of the newspaper/broadcast ban this sentiment seems eerily prophetic, coming as it did even before the rule was proposed or *Red Lion* decided. It was echoed just recently by Justice Souter, however, in a case that turned on the vanishing distinctions among electronic media: "[B]ecause we know that changes in these regulated technologies will enormously alter the structure of regulation itself, we should be shy about saying the final word today about what will be accepted as reasonable tomorrow." *Denver Area Educ. Telecommunications Consortium, Inc. v. FCC*, 116 S. Ct. 2374, 2402 (1996) (Souter, J., concurring).

[115]1985 Fairness Report, *supra* note 54 at 147.

[116]*Id.* at 154, n.39 (emphasis added). As this publication was going to press, Senate Commerce Committee Chairman John McCain (R-Ariz.) introduced a bill to repeal the newspaper/broadcast cross ownership rule, calling it "one of the most archaic provisions remaining in telecommunications law." Sen. Ernest F. Hollings (D-S.C.) was expected to oppose the repeal effort. *McCain Bill Would End Cross Ownership Ban,* BROADCASTING & CABLE, April 28, 1997 at 6.

Index

The Author: **Richard T. Kaplar** is Vice President of The Media Institute in Washington, D.C. He has written, edited, or produced over 35 books and monographs on a variety of communications policy topics with an emphasis on First Amendment issues and government regulation of the media. Mr. Kaplar is the author of *Advertising Rights: The Neglected Freedom* and *Prime Time for Repeal: The Financial Interest and Syndication Rules*; co-author of *The Government Factor: Undermining Journalistic Ethics in the Information Age;* and editor of *The First Amendment and the Media – 1997* and *Bad Prescription for the First Amendment.*

Laurence H. Winer is a Professor of Law at the Arizona State University College of Law, specializing in media law, constitutional law, and legal ethics. His latest work is "Children Are Not a Constitutional Blank Check" in *Rationales & Rationalizations: Regulating the Electronic Media* (The Media Institute, 1997). Prof. Winer received his Ph.D. in mathematics from Boston University and law degree from Yale Law School. He serves on The Media Institute's First Amendment Advisory Council and on the Editorial Board of the JURIMETRICS JOURNAL OF LAW, SCIENCE AND TECHNOLOGY.

Cross Ownership at the Crossroads was produced by Alan Moseley. Gaylen O'Leary provided research assistance.

The Media Institute is a nonprofit research foundation specializing in communications policy and First Amendment issues. The Institute exists to advocate and encourage freedom of speech, a competitive communications industry, and excellence in journalism.

Founded in 1979, The Media Institute pursues a program agenda that encompasses virtually all sectors of the media, ranging from traditional print and broadcast outlets to contemporary entrants such as cable, satellites, and interactive networks.

The Institute publishes books and monographs, prepares regulatory filings and court briefs, convenes conferences, and sponsors a luncheon series in Washington for journalists and communications executives.

Since its inception, the Institute has been an independent advocate of a robust press and a dynamic communications industry. The organization has evolved into one of the country's leading "think tanks" focusing on the First Amendment and communications policy.

The Media Institute has examined the newspaper/broadcast cross ownership restriction in two previous publications, *The Diversity Principle: Friend or Foe of the First Amendment?* (see below), and a paper prepared for the Bush Administration transition team (with the Freedom of Expression Foundation).

To support the work of the Institute, or for further information, contact Patrick D. Maines, President, at the address below.

Also of interest:

Rationales & Rationalizations: Regulating the Electronic Media, seven essays on traditional and new regulatory rationales, including scarcity, public forum, children's well-being, market failure, and "voluntary" self regulation. With an introduction by Sen. Patrick J. Leahy.

The First Amendment and the Media—1997, updates on government actions in 27 issue areas affecting First Amendment rights in broadcasting, cable, on-line services, commercial speech, and print media.

The Diversity Principle: Friend or Foe of the First Amendment? details how the diversity principle has been misapplied to broadcasting, cable TV, and the telecommunications industry.

Speaking Freely: The Public Interest in Unfettered Speech, five essays on broadcast content controls regarding violence, indecency, children's TV, commercial speech, and the Fairness Doctrine.

For information about these and other publications, contact the Publications Department at the addresses or numbers below.

The Media Institute
Suite 301, 1000 Potomac Street, N.W., Washington, D.C. 20007
Phone: 202-298-7512 • Fax: 202-337-7092 • E-Mail: tmi@clark.net

Visit The Media Institute on the World Wide Web at http://www.mediainst.org